THE ACCIDENTAL FOREIGN CORRESPONDENT

The Accidental Foreign Correspondent

KIERAN COOKE

Kilsallagh
Press

First published July 2022
Kilsallagh Press

ISBN 978-1-7397446-0-1

Edited by David Clare
Cover & book design: John Houston

> **"ALL OF HUMANITY'S PROBLEMS STEM FROM MAN'S INABILITY TO SIT QUIETLY IN A ROOM ALONE."**
>
> *Blaise Pascal*

Contents

Pictures

ix

Introduction

Missing the Six Day War · Chance is a fine thing
A falling coconut points the way · Transient fame written in stone

xi

Chapter 1: China & Hong Kong

A kite-buying mission · Skulduggery in the duck down business
Mao cracks a joke · The mysterious Mr Feng

1

Chapter 2: The London years

Sausage rolls stop the world · A holy hijacking
Lilliburlero no more · Fishnets and sequins in Soho

14

Chapter 3: The UN & New York

A pen for Mrs Marcos · The Assembly nosepicker
Tears flow for Brezhnev · Brendan gives Columbus a kicking

33

Chapter 4: Indonesia

An excitable monkey · The dangers of pooting
A man out of Conrad · Hand in hand with an amorous orangutan
Transvestites and Champagne corks

40

Chapter 5: The Levant

A freckled beauty · The laughing poet · An elegant revolutionary
Sailing with the Patriarch · Massacre at the synagogue
Nik the fixer

59

Chapter 6: Albania

Communism gets a facelift · A sexy saxophone
Taking the slow train · A monarch for months

85

Chapter 7: Libya
Gadaffi in the desert • The leader's bed chamber
On military parade • A war is lost
Bang goes the Bulgar • A gift for controversy
97

Chapter 8: The Papal trail
Nearly a priest • The Papa talks pidgin • Mass with Fidel and Che
Red socks in Rome • Ordained at last
111

Chapter 9: Ireland
Shoot-out at the cemetery • Tea with the Taoiseach
The airport hearse • Charlie dreams in Morse
Wittgenstein's puzzled chickens
125

Chapter 10: Fine dining, strange smells
A fish head for Miss Marple • Lunch with Goldilocks
Dinner at the palace • Blancmange in a lavatory
The sniffer dog goes wild
145

Chapter 11. Close Shaves
Tear gas in paradise • A pole dancer puts the boot in
Laughing in the face of danger
163

Chapter 12: And the closing headlines . . .
174

Acknowledgements
176

Pictures

Cover image
Aftermath of battle, Aouzou Strip, Libya-Chad border, 1987 - Kieran Cooke on assignment (unidentified photographer)

Introduction
Warning! Coconuts above! (Swaminathan/Flickr)

Chapter 1
Strings of beautiful Chinese kites (Agnieszka Ziomek/Unsplash)

Chapter 2
Bush House in all its splendour (BBC Archive);
Meard Street Mary, Soho, London 1981 (Lesley Nelson)

Chapter 3
KC tries to lighten the UN gloom, New York 1982 (unidentified photographer)

Chapter 4
An orangutan's look of love (Kevin Schofield/Flickr)

Chapter 5
Aegina harbour in the early 1980s (Andrea-44/Flickr);
Katerina Anghelaki-Rooke, poet and storyteller (Kieran Cooke); political radical Maria Becket (photo courtesy Daphne Becket)

Chapter 6
KC checking up on Hoxha's whereabouts (Kerin Hope)

Chapter 7
Muammar Gadaffi liked to call the shots (NAVY/Wikimedia Commons)

Chapter 8
Pope John Paul comes down to Earth; and in Papua New Guinea (unidentified photographers)

Chapter 9
A homely welcome in County Mayo (Diego Sideburns/Flickr);
Wittgenstein lived here – in Little Killary (Kieran Cooke)

Chapter 10
Hands-on approach to fish-head curry (Mark Hitchcock/Flickr)

Chapter 11
The terror of tear gas (Wikimedia Commons)

Chapter 12
Missing the magic of Nina Simone (unidentified photographer)

Acknowledgements
'KC at work on Mykonos, Greece, 1988 (unidentified photographer)

Introduction

Missing the Six Day War • Chance is a fine thing
A falling coconut points the way • Transient fame written in stone

The two Mirage jets do a belly roll as they scream over the ship: they look like playful dolphins, their silver skins etched against a cloudless blue sky.

It's 9am on June 5th, 1967, and what was to become known as the Six Day War is beginning.

The ship, a Turkish rust bucket spewing clouds of black smoke and smelling of a mix of rotting fruit and soap powder, had belched its way out of the port of Haifa in northern Israel late the night before, bound for Istanbul.

The few passengers on board form an anxious huddle. A pale Dane wonders if we are about to be bombed. An American with a head of hair like a giant black halo talks of returning to Israel to join in the fighting.

The crew smoke and spit husks of sunflower seeds about the deck, indifferent to the drama unfolding not far away.

I'm angst-ridden, cursing my foolishness.

A year before, just prior to coming to Israel, I – an 18-year-old with journalistic pretensions – had visited a kindly man dressed in a holey cardigan in a dimly-lit office at what was then *The Manchester Guardian.* "Drop us a line if you come across anything interesting," he'd said.

Just before boarding in Haifa, I'd posted a long piece to Manchester. A game of charades was being acted out in the Middle East, I'd written. The Israelis, Egyptians and Syrians were engaged in a phantom war. Despite all the bellicose talk, nothing was going to happen.

The Mirages flew back over us. By the time we ducked and covered our ears, they were out of sight.

The piece, of course, was never published. Maybe, in the confusion of war, it never left Israel. But it wasn't a promising start to a career in journalism.

School hadn't been a success, but a young London vicar, who worked part-time for the United Nations Association, ran a scheme that sent footless young students abroad to teach English. A group of four of us ended up at a kibbutz in Israel.

Life at the settlement bordering the Negev desert wasn't easy. The kibbutz was run on strictly socialist lines, with spartan accommodation and basic food.

There were several native English speakers at the settlement and our proposed lessons came to nothing. Instead, in return for our keep, we were up at daybreak, put to work in the orchards or shoveling muck in the chicken sheds.

A number of holocaust survivors, most of Polish origin, lived on the kibbutz. When clothes were sent to the laundry they were named, never numbered. I was given the name Mordechai. Somewhere, there's an old, threadbare shirt with the Hebrew script stretched round its collar.

Every so often a party of Jewish students would arrive from New York for a few weeks stay. They'd complain about the food, pine for their mothers and take issue with the stern kibbutz work ethic.

"You think I'm going to bust my ass picking lemons? Forget it," said Saul from the Bronx.

There were upsides to life in the desert.

Naomi, a fiercely proud native-born Israeli or Sabra – the word means prickly pear in Hebrew – taught me Jewish lullabies.

She was a part-time soldier, had a boyfriend serving on the Syrian border, and felt it her patriotic duty to convert me – a Catholic boy from far away – to the virtues of the Zionist cause.

After a year of kibbutz life, I caught the boat to Istanbul. At 19, I knew how to prune apple trees and do the hora wedding dance, but not much else. Back in England, I went back to studying, still – despite the debacle over *The Manchester Guardian* article – intent on a reporter's career.

The only institution willing to accept my minimal qualifications was Hull University and the one course with spare capacity was Southeast Asian studies.

I didn't have much idea where Hull was, let alone Southeast Asia.

The smell of Hull's fish docks – still just about alive back then – wafted through the air as a petite Javanese lady, swaddled in blankets against the cold northern winds, struggled to teach a small group of us *Bahasa Indonesia*, a lingua franca dialect of Malay and the official language of the Indonesian archipelago.

The poet Philip Larkin, in charge of the university's library in those days, once gently reprimanded me for mislaying a book on Balinese spirit worship.

After Hull, I set off to see the East. The money quickly ran out: the plan was to go on and work in Australia, but fate stepped in.

Sitting outside a restaurant in northern Thailand, a falling coconut came within inches of crushing the cranium of a fellow diner.

A few months earlier, I'd been walking along the beach in Aldeburgh, Suffolk, with my sister Ailsa. An elderly woman in stout brogues and tweed skirt had gone striding by.

"That's Imogen Holst, the composer and singer," said Ailsa.

Ted Holst, the man who escaped death by coconut, was a cousin of Imogen and a descendant of Gustav, of *The Planets* fame. That sort of happenstance tends to encourage lively conversation.

Ted, who was to become a lifelong friend, was living in Japan. I decided to ditch Sydney in favour of Tokyo.

Teaching English in Japan, I told my students of the coconut incident. After class, an elderly woman approached me.

She and her English husband had been living in Japan when World War II broke out. For several years, he'd been interned in a camp in the hills outside Tokyo. A few days after being released, he was taking a walk in the countryside when a US military plane flew over, dropping emergency supplies.

A coconut didn't kill him: the poor man was squashed by a pallet laden with cans of SPAM pork luncheon meat.

After a time in Japan, I'd gone to visit friends in Hong Kong. They suggested I go to see a consultant about a troublesome eye condition.

"Oh dear," he said. "This is serious – we'll have to operate."

I should have been suspicious. The consultant had a nasally posh Dublin southside accent, perfumed hands, and a surgery stuffed full of Chinese antiques.

The operation – it was later found to have been unnecessary – was eye-wateringly expensive.

Forced to look for a job locally, I produced some yellowing old articles written as a student and bluffed my way into working as a reporter for the local government-controlled radio station.

All of a sudden, I was a journalist.

A haphazard career unfolded, much of it reflected in these tales.

Many of the pieces in this book are light in tone. This is not to suggest a reporter's job is full of fun. Far from it. There have been dark times and a few close shaves.

What I hope these pages illustrate is the often bizarre and random nature of events, and the humour that sometimes accompanies them – even in the most dire circumstances.

My last proper job – in the way of being permanent, pensionable and respectable – was with BBC World Service radio way back in the early 1980s. For the rest of the time, I've been freelance.

Freelancers like to see themselves as the swashbuckling crack troops of journalism. The staffers can sit in their luxury hotels, fiddling with their expense accounts, or jet in to steal the big stories, but we are the ones who go out on the frontline, feel the pulse of a nation, really know what's going on.

The reality is a little different. In many ways, freelancers are their own worst enemies – dilettantes who refuse to conform to the system, valuing their freedom above all else. They – we – are grossly, almost laughably, underpaid.

On my first foreign assignment in Indonesia, other correspondents would arrive at press conferences in chauffeur-driven, air-conditioned cars, whereas I had to depend on the bus or a rattling old taxi.

Staffers had servants in their houses; I had mosquitoes.

Then there was the frustration of dealing with news desks back home. I once rang in to complain about the non-appearance in the newspaper of a story I'd laboured over for days.

"Oh, you know how it is, Kieran – something far more boring came along," said the night editor.

Despite all that, I wouldn't have had it any other way. Life's been rich – and varied.

In between reporting assignments, there's been a spell as a disc jockey in northern Thailand, a drive in a vintage car across the US, and a brief and inglorious attempt at joining a tap dancing team in Dublin.

Very few professions allow you to see so many places and, more importantly, meet and talk to everyone from popes to pole dancers, wealthy financiers to down and outs, saintly characters to criminals, celebrities to ordinary Joes and Josephines. Everyone has a story.

There have been a few fillips along the way.

Alistair Cooke, who broadcast his '*Letter from America*' for the BBC for nearly 60 years, once wrote me a note on a postcard – it pictured himself – saying he enjoyed listening to his namesake on the wireless. He then went on to politely point out one or two errors in my scripts.

"Should I go on bended knee?" asked Mrs Thatcher when I was introduced to her as the *Financial Times* correspondent during a prime ministerial visit to Indonesia. Her low, silky, vaguely threatening voice had shades of a leather-clad dominatrix about it.

For a number of years, a large granite slab stood outside the venerable old Galle Face Hotel in Colombo, Sri Lanka, listing the names of various prominent people who had stayed in its ornate but fusty rooms.

The roll call included Louis Mountbatten, Gregory Peck, Yuri Gagarin, Ursula Andress and George Bernard Shaw, plus a sprinkling of royalty and a drizzle of US presidents.

During a stay at the hotel, I wrote an article about a 'Miss Photogenic' beauty contest held there, a colourful occasion featuring long-legged girls in belt-like skirts. There were frequent crashes as distracted elderly waiters, mostly retirees from the Sri Lankan armed forces, dropped plates of jackfruit curry.

The hotel's owner thought the piece amusing and had me inscribed – name misspelt – on the granite tablet, squeezed between Robert Burns and Arthur C. Clarke.

Fame is transient, especially in journalism.

Mrs Thatcher did not, of course, bend her knee but moved smartly on. The granite slab at the Galle Face has disappeared – along with a colony of rodents that used to haunt the hotel dining room. Indira Gandhi, Laurence Olivier and myself have probably been smashed into pieces of hardcore.

The journalist Murray Sayle became a Fleet Street legend in the 1960s and 70s, famous for scoops that included tracking down Che Guevara in the jungles of Bolivia and finding the spy Kim Philby pondering over his corporate dividend cheques in a Moscow post office.

Sayle said there were only two basic story lines in journalism: "We name the guilty men" and "Arrow points to defective part".

Shock also plays an important role – what a BBC newsroom colleague referred to as those sudden, magical "Cor, fuck me!" moments.

V.S. Naipaul, in *A House for Mr Biswas*, describes the travails of an aspiring journalist.

Biswas, the book's main character, finds himself jobless, living in a hut where copies of the local *Trinidad Sentinel* newspaper serve as wallpaper.

He notices that each news story starts with the same words: "Amazing scenes were witnessed yesterday when…"

Biswas writes to the editor, begins his sample story in similar fashion to those on the wallpaper – and becomes a journalist.

Many of these stories could start in a similar vein.

I hope you enjoy them.

Kieran Cooke
Co Mayo, Ireland, 2022

Chapter 1

Hong Kong and China

A kite-buying mission • Skulduggery in the duck down business
Mao cracks a joke • The mysterious Mr Feng

All manner of fortune hunters and expatriate oddballs – including wannabe journalists – washed up in Hong Kong in the 1970s. The colony was like one big transit lounge.

The colonial establishment, dominated by a straight-laced brand of Scottish masonic conservatism, went about governing while the rest of the population concentrated on the serious business of making money. Hong Kong always had tremendous energy and bustle about it, but in many ways it was a small town, inward looking with provincial attitudes.

The Vietnam War was entering its final dramatic phase just down the road, but in Hong Kong it was blocked drains and the proceedings at the local council that led the news agenda.

The early morning radio host – a Shakespearean actor who had missed the plane home when the rest of the touring company left – would take calls from colonial ladies about lost budgerigars or neglectful bin men.

1

It was a territory locked off from its hinterland; China was a looming presence on the horizon, but, back then, strictly out of bounds.

Then, in 1976, Mao Tse Tung died. The great upheaval of the Cultural Revolution was declared over. The first signs of a possible opening up of China appeared.

Brendan, the brother, provided the opportunity for breaking through the bamboo curtain. An entrepreneur living in California, he'd set up a leisure company specialising in kites.

With the aid of some headed notepaper and a post office box address, I was transformed from journalist to international trader, eager to make a killing in the China kite market.

The Canton, or Guangzhou, Trade Fair was held each autumn, the Middle Kingdom's shop window to the world.

The great kite-buying expedition
China, September 1977

The trip to Canton does not start well. A group of us – real-time traders along with pretend businesspeople – were gathered at the scruffy, single-storey China border post, precious visas in hand.

"Hey, look at that cute Red Guard," says the wife of a US grain merchant. She manoeuvres a backside the size of a Great Plains hay barn out of the doorway, camera at the ready.

The border guard, kitted out in a uniform washed and bleached within an inch of its life, lifts an ancient-looking rifle. The Union Jack hanging limply from a pole on the other side of the border suddenly looks a long way away.

Our minder, Comrade Wang, intervenes. "Foreign friends are not allowed to take photos without permission," he announces firmly. A fetid odour fills the air. Wang has atrocious breath.

Dental care is not a priority in China. Mao Tse Tung had terrible teeth; according to his doctor, there was nothing the Great Helmsman enjoyed more in his final years than sitting in his armchair, surrounded by the latest batch of Red Army beauties, gnawing on pieces of fatty pork with his blackened, broken stumps.

Wang is like an Englishman abroad, deciding that the best way of dealing with foreigners is coming up close and shouting.

"You are very welcome to the China, friend Cookie," says Wang. It is like being slapped in the face with a dead seal.

Wang has assigned himself as my personal minder. He follows me into the toilet – any need for privacy is regarded with deep suspicion.

"Ah," says Wang. "You are very span and spit, friend Cookie."

Food is served in the border post canteen. Places are set aside for various religions.

"Are you a Muslim?" a stern woman handing out plates enquires of a shirt buyer from Seattle.

"No," he says. "I'm an alcoholic."

We rattle along on the train – all deep seats and antimacassars – to Canton. Mao-suited attendants serve strong brown tea out of battered flasks. The smell of mothballs overpowers the halitosis; it's as if China is a big old chest, its lid creaking open.

Comrade Wang, who insists on sitting by me, is not all he seems. "You are perhaps not only interested in the kites?" he asks. "I think you are a writer? It is good to use the words."

Ten minutes into China and I've been rumbled. I feel like a schoolboy caught making rude gestures behind teacher's back.

Wang does not seem to mind. The only punishment for my charade is a half-hour lecture on the great happiness of the people under Marxist Leninist Mao Tse Tung thought.

At 10am the next day, the world's traders, all hungry for a deal with China, gather in the cavernous entrance hall of the fair complex. Bundles of red balloons bump and argue with each other on the ceiling. Giant portraits of Marx, Engels, Lenin, Stalin and Mao hang on the walls.

Marx looks glum, as if he's just missed the last bus home. Engels is haughty. Lenin has toothache. Stalin's smile carries a not-so-subtle threat. Only Mao looks jolly – cheeky and cherubic.

The story goes that Chinese officials, in an attempt to show Mao was blessed with a subtle sense of humour, had, a few years before, gathered the media together for a question and answer session.

"Oh, great leader," asked one journalist, "what do you think would have happened if Khrushchev had been assassinated and not Kennedy?"

Mao thought for a while, playing with the mole on his white, smooth cheek.

"I do not think Aristotle Onassis would have married Mrs Khrushchev," came the reply.

The loudspeakers screech out their messages of welcome.

"Eternal friendship between our peoples. Together we will build in peace a glorious future."

Trade deals in Canton are based on a 'first come, first served' basis. Find the right room and official and you're virtually home and dry. Prices are fixed – and generally much lower than in other countries. Being ahead of the posse is vital.

This winner-takes-all approach leads to a great deal of jostling and indecorous pushing at the opening ceremony.

One of the most sought-after goods this year is duck down: the world is crying out for duvets and feather-filled jackets.

The trouble is there are not enough feathers to go round. Only China – with millions of ducks happily quacking their way through the rice paddies – has feathers in abundance.

Feathers are sold by weight – spray on a light film of water and the weight, along with the price, goes up significantly. Or maybe a trader might mix in some heavier chicken feathers with the lightweight duck down. You have to be eagle-eyed in the feather business – and fast on your feet.

The speeches finish and the ribbon is cut. Among the first group of traders across the start line are three feather merchants from New York's Lower East Side.

They are sweating and carrying a little too much weight as they lead the charge through the maze of trade fair walkways, making a bee line for the office of the chief duck down salesman. At first, they waddle, then they break into a run.

Their suits are shiny, with trousers that end six inches above their tasseled shoes.

One, a short-sighted member of the trio, tries to outflank his colleagues by taking a short cut across the hall. We watch as he falls headlong into a cunningly-disguised ornamental pond.

"What the fuck?" echoes round the hall. A group of pale-looking Czech traders – tractor buyers from Prague – hurry on past.

Next morning at breakfast, the winner of the duck down derby is holding court and doing deals. There is news that his fellow buyer has sprained an ankle and returned to Hong Kong, abject and featherless.

My own buying operations pass off remarkably smoothly. A man with round tortoiseshell glasses with lenses like the bottom of Coca-Cola bottles – and breath you could cut with a chainsaw – does some magic fluttering calculations on his abacus.

Stand aside Messrs Guggenheim and Rothschild – the king of the traders has arrived.

I buy 12,000 kites – gloriously-coloured butterflies, peacocks, dragons, grasshoppers and bumble bees – for US$6,000. Included are quantities of string and multiple wooden spools.

In fact, mine is believed to be the lowest-priced order ever placed by a US company at the fair. Comrade Abacus is not impressed. I offer my hand to shake on the deal, but he brushes it aside as if it's a contaminated object.

Fellow traders, whether actual wheeler-dealers or, like me, in Canton on vaguely false pretences, are a varied bunch. There are stern-looking toiletware buyers from Moscow, lavishly-robed cotton merchants from Lagos, and shoe purchasers from Damascus.

A large Australian, here to investigate buying dentists' chairs, yearns for a meat pie.

"No bloody decent tucker around here mate. Spaghetti and rice is all you get."

Herbie and Al, from northern California, describe themselves as buyers of light industrial products. Lubricated with a few drinks, it turns out Herbie is after bamboo drum sets, while Al is investigating sourcing his dildo manufacturing operations in China.

A blond-haired man from Boston walks about in tennis whites, a racquet tucked like a swagger stick under his arm. He doesn't seem to be buying anything – he's just out for what he calls "a China playing experience".

The buyer from a giant US chemical corporation struggles with his chopsticks at the communal dinner table.

"Back at HQ in Michigan they say I cover pole to pole, Guam to Afghanistan," he says, dropping a piece of fried bean curd into his lap.

Someone asks how the US chemical industry is dealing with the adverse publicity caused by the use of its products during the Vietnam War.

"You mean the Agent Orange business? Just a passing storm. Our reputation is still good."

His German wife is a veteran of several China trips. She has the no-nonsense manner of a headmistress.

"I always bring supplies of toilet paper and also of light bulbs.

"It is good to spray down the bed and in the corners of the rooms for the insects. And you must never be naked in the room. The staff will come in at any time."

She warms to her theme.

"If you lock the door you are reported to be a spy. And if you are seen without the clothes you will be told it is immoral behaviour and maybe you will be deported."

It's true. All visitors to Canton are accommodated in the

Dong Fang hotel, a large grey tomb of a building, its rooms dimly lit and musty.

Your attendant – there's one guarding every few rooms – enters at any time of the day or night. The alleged purpose of these visitations is to replenish tea supplies.

A big cork stopper is pulled from a flask and the room's teapot is refilled. He or she then looks diligently round to check for any stray anti-revolutionaries or "capitalist roaders" bowing to bourgeois tendencies who might have sneaked in. There is no banter, certainly no "Have a nice day".

A couple from San Francisco are buying jade. She wears large, looping earrings and a flowing kaftan. He's all in Levis, a long, yellowing moustache draped like dripping custard down each side of his mouth. The scent of patchouli oil fills the air.

Beside purchasing jade, they have another mission: they are out to convert Chinese officials to the latest California therapy fad, which involves groups of naked people laying on the ground and slowly slithering towards each other.

They show their hosts a book of photos. "It instils calmness and a very different form of togetherness," says the kaftan woman.

China is not ready for therapy – certainly not of the naked kind. The two are quickly escorted back to the Hong Kong border.

Various excursions to show off the achievements of Maoist China are laid on for the visiting foreign friends.

In the West, acupuncture is becoming increasingly popular. Several visiting specialists in alternative medicine are in Canton.

A friend, a Mandarin speaker, had accompanied a group of young American medics to a clinic in Shanghai. The medics were shown into a small room; an elderly man in his pyjamas was ushered in, needles inserted into his legs and forearms.

"What exactly is this patient being treated for?" asked one of the group.

Translations go back and forth. Finally, the medical attendant stepped forward.

"This person is being treated for chronic constipation."

The visiting medics made a scrabble for the door.

We're also offered an acupuncture experience. Like birds on a greenhouse roof, we perch around a glass bubble immediately above a hospital operating theatre.

"They're showing off again," says the Australian dental equipment buyer. Still yearning for his meat pie, he's in a bad mood.

"I've seen it all before – think they can do wonders with their bloody needles. All snake oil science if you ask me."

A curtain is pulled back to reveal, stretched out below, a man with his rib cage wide open. Bloodied organs pump away. Arms, legs and shoulders are full of needles.

The patient is fully conscious, probably truamatised more by the array of foreign faces staring down at him than the operation he's undergoing.

The door of the operating theatre opens onto a scruffy patch of grass. A big battered kettle simmers on a gas hob. It all seems very relaxed. The surgeon is sipping tea.

A great weight suddenly pushes me head down onto the glass bubble. The Australian has fainted and fallen on top of me.

For a second, I picture myself and the meat pie man crashing through the glass, to be skewered on the patient's rib cage below.

A minder intervenes. The Australian is led away, wobbly and unusually silent. I'm given a restorative glass of thick brown tea.

The other entertainment laid on for us is a football match between the visiting businessmen and the hotel staff.

The business team is dominated by Germans – most of them bulky men from the Ruhr, metal buyers and machine tool engineers.

Tommaso is from Turin. He's in Canton representing two Italian companies. For one, he is purchasing quantities of fabrics for wedding dresses. For the other, he's buying manhole covers.

He fancies himself as something of a footballing wizard, but

– along with me – he's been left on the substitutes bench by the Germans.

Thousands of locals have gathered – or been dragooned – to watch the game in the city's main football stadium. They are very orderly – and quiet.

The visitors rush like raging bulls about the pitch. The man from Krupp races down the touchline, barges into a chef and floors a room boy before passing to the buyer from Bayer, who boots the ball into the net. The crowd clap politely.

The foreigners knock in three more goals, but quickly run out of steam. Bratwurst and sauerkraut-filled bodies are not designed to run about in the sweaty heat of southern China.

The hotel players begin to tap the ball about the pitch as the Germans slow to a crawl. With full time looming, it's three goals each.

Tommaso and I are finally allowed on. He gains the ball, artfully nutmegs the hotel receptionist, but then, approaching the goal, falls headlong. He hobbles off, injured.

The hotel staff, now dominating the game, seem reluctant to score a winner. The final whistle is blown. An honorable draw is declared. I have not touched the ball.

On our last evening in Canton, a group of us gather in one of the hotel's larger rooms used as the unofficial HQ for US traders. There is beer, an acidic, locally-made champagne called Pink Cockatoo and – most lethal of all – Chinese Maotai, a sorghum-based, jet-propelling liquor.

A party gets underway. The non-Muslim alcoholic shirt buyer from Seattle is there: he demands silence and stands to recite *The Shooting of Dan McGrew*. There's plenty of passion, but after three verses he loses his way, collapses in a chair and goes to sleep.

The Canton-based consul of Poland and his wife have been invited along.

He has long hair, a gentle, thoughtful way about him, and

plays the guitar badly. She has skin like alabaster and moves with the elegance of a ballerina. She teaches me to say '*latawiec*' – the Polish word for kite.

"Now you know my language," she says. Her laugh is like a breeze blowing through the most delicate of chandeliers.

We sing – gloriously out of tune – Dylan, Cohen and The Beatles.

There's an interruption. A Chinese official glides in, ever so quietly.

Our visitor, Mr Feng, is the height of elegance, his Mao suit carefully tailored and ironed, its buttons shining, its texture brushed. He wears slip-on black shoes of soft leather. The hair is fashionably trimmed, the complexion unblemished, the breath odourless.

"Please," he says. "Carry on – it seems like an interesting party." He sits himself down on the arm of a chair, leg nonchalantly dangling in mid air.

Uniforms tend to have an instant sobering effect on even the most drunken of gatherings.

"Who is he?" whispers the Polish consul. "In my time here I have never seen anyone like this."

Feng seems to know us all. Tom, a publisher from Chicago, is asked about his future business plans. Hans, a Hong Kong German diplomat and rather obvious spook, is questioned about his recent trip to Beijing.

Our respective countries are discussed. Feng is particularly knowledgeable on Hong Kong's streets and restaurants, though he says he's never visited the city.

"We in China are still very underdeveloped," he says. "We have a lot of catching up to do."

This is heresy. Mao Tse Tung thought does not allow for any criticism of the established order. There's certainly no public admission of lagging behind the West.

Maybe a trap is being set. We don't know whether to nod or

shake heads in disagreement. Feng turns to me.

"And you must be the kite man?" he enquires. "You must also be observing and finding it interesting?"

Halitosis Wang is obviously not the only one in the know about my other life as a journalist.

A few more words are exchanged. Our visitor raises an arm in a priestly wave of farewell. We all – except for the slumbering shirt man – rise and bow.

Next day, the train ride back to the Hong Kong border has an end-of-term atmosphere about it.

"I tell my husband this is the last time," says the wife of the US chemical man. "I am not made for such places. In future, he can come here alone."

Her husband is disgruntled and deal-less.

"Goddamned Swiss beat me to it. Those Yuropeens sit in miserable hotel rooms for months, eating rubbish food and giving themselves ulcers waiting to seal an agreement. You won't find me leading that kind of life."

Our group is still in recovery mode from the previous night's party. The Seattle shirt man has a bluish tinge about the jowls. The blond Bostonian walks by, still clutching his tennis racquet.

A railway official comes down the carriage, holding up a copy of *Playboy*, opened to its centre-spread.

You cannot throw away anything in China. Leave an empty tube of toothpaste in Beijing and it will follow you about the country.

"Room 323. Who is staying in this room?" The tone is disdainful, faintly accusatory.

Racquet man gingerly raises his hand. The official approaches and drops the offending item into the tennis player's lap. We all cheer. Even the railway man breaks into a smile.

The great China kite-buying mission is over.

Postscript

When the Canton kite-buying trip took place, the dust was still settling in the aftermath of what had been an intense power struggle in China.

On one side were those who wanted more Cultural Revolution-style upheaval – including Jiang Qing, Mao's actor wife. On the other were those seeking market reforms and a gradual opening up of the country.

In the end, the reformers won and China started on a breathless period of growth, giving birth to today's odd mixture – a tightly-controlled communist system ruling over a thoroughly capitalist society in which Mao, whose policies were responsible for the deaths of millions, is still revered.

In an odd historical twist, Hong Kong – in the 1970s, seemingly entirely devoted to money making and strictly apolitical – is now going through its own cultural revolution, with residents battling against being swallowed up by Beijing.

The border post and its ramshackle set of single-storey buildings has long since disappeared, the land it stood on absorbed into the sprawling metropolis of Shenzhen, now a city of 13 million.

The old school of China traders is no more. Gone are the entrepreneurs who were willing to put up with shoddy hostels and uncertain food in order to do deals – like the pale-faced Dane I met who spent months traipsing round hospitals and clinics in China, buying up afterbirth for use in beauty products in the West.

Gone too is the idealism of many of the early visitors to Mao's China. A Breton friend – on the barricades during the student riots and general strike in France in 1968 – went off to China to learn about Maoist ways.

He emerged a few years later a thorough capitalist, setting up a business supplying women in the West with Chinese-made silk bras and thongs.

The kite business euphoria did not last long.

It's one of the fundamental rules of trading: buy an item for $100, sell it for $150, and you make a worthwhile profit; buy something for 50 cents and even if you sell it for 10 times that amount you still haven't made yourself rich.

I gave up business and returned to journalism. Quantities of kites were sold, but a great many mouldered away in my brother's California garage.

The Polish Consul and his beautiful wife were not seen again; I've yet to go to Poland and try out my one-word vocabulary.

The mysterious Mr Feng did reappear.

A friend who had attended the Canton party was in Beijing on a diplomatic mission some years later. A high-level meeting was arranged with China's deputy minister of security.

The friend was ushered into a large, modern office and there, behind an immaculately-polished desk, was Feng.

"And how is the kite man?" he asked.

CHAPTER 2:
The London years

Sausage rolls stop the world • A holy hijacking
Lilliburlero no more • Fishnets and sequins in Soho

It's four o'clock in the morning in the basement canteen of Bush House, for more than 70 years the London home of the BBC World Service.

The fried eggs, cooked hours before, have a congealed, glazed look about them, yokes the eyes of jaundiced fish.

A recently-returned foreign correspondent is talking about his time overseas.

"You know what I most disliked about being out there?" A piece of fried bread is waved in the general direction of the outside world.

His table companion, a senior editor, is concentrating on cutting through a soggy slice of Welsh Rarebit.

"You know what it was? I'll tell you – it was being surrounded by all those bloody foreigners."

After five years in Hong Kong and Japan, I'm back in London, and fate – plus a bit of luck – has landed me a job at the BBC.

Last Tango in Paris – it had never made it to Hong Kong – is showing at the cinema, but the times don't suit. So instead, from a phone box outside the Ritz hotel, I answer an advert in the *UK Press Gazette* for summer relief work in the newsroom at Bush House. An entry test is arranged.

In the late 1970s, groups of Australians, having done their European tour, would line up their VW camper vans for sale on Sunday mornings in the small alley separating Bush House from the Australian High Commission next door.

The entrepreneurial Aussies were rumoured to also sell current copies of the BBC's editorial examination.

I got the job and spent four years in the World Service newsroom – my last full-time, salaried and pensionable job.

Bush days and nights
1978-1982

Walk down Kingsway in central London, then through the imposing portico of Bush House (simply 'Bush' to its insiders), and you enter another world – or worlds. Exotic women from Bucharest and Bulawayo; gruff Serbian translators warring with their Croatian counterparts; heavy-set men from Moscow cloistered in corners.

Life at the BBC World Service was a mix of the extraordinary and the mundane.

Hours would be spent writing about the rise of Ayatollah Khomeini and the Teheran hostage crisis, the Vietnamese invasion of Cambodia, the Soviet occupation of Afghanistan, the assassination of Egypt's President Sadat, and the dust-up in the Falklands.

Then, shift completed, it was out onto the Strand and the bus or tube home.

In between revolutions and coups, the refreshments trolley would arrive in the newsroom, and the world's problems would be temporarily put on hold: getting hold of a sausage roll was, for the moment at least, far more important than the battle for Kabul.

Inhabitants of the newsroom were thoroughly professional, but cultivated an air of *sangfroid*; heaven forbid anything or anybody be seen to be taken too seriously. Rushing about or betraying a sense of panic was deeply frowned upon.

"The Pope has been shot – this will now move to the top of the bulletin," an editor would announce, crossword temporarily interrupted.

There were specialists on any number of subjects. A smiling, quietly-spoken Scottish woman had worked as a code breaker during World War II. A man with a pipe permanently jammed between yellow teeth would mutter about the latest developments in the Balkans.

There was also some unpleasant chicanery going on.

Shortly before I joined, Georgi Markov, a Bulgarian dissident working at Bush, was waiting for a bus on Waterloo Bridge when he was stabbed in the leg with poison from a specially-adapted umbrella. He died four days later: the Bulgarian secret service or Soviet KGB were widely suspected of being behind the killing.

Back then, union rules forbade journalists from using newly-installed computers. Instead, stories were dictated to typists, each one with their own set of eccentricities.

An elderly gent always wore blazer and bow tie: in between bouts on the typewriter, he'd sound off on his two great passions – Puccini operas and cockapoo crossbreed dogs.

One typist dressed as if she was off to a concert, complete with feather boa and heavy make-up.

"I came across this gorgeous man in the National Gallery," she tells me in the midst of typing a news story on a government shake-up in Zambia. "He had such wonderful cheekbones, but then I found out he was from New Zealand. You have to draw the line somewhere, don't you darling?"

Newsreaders were the calmest of people. Some were actors

filling in between parts. Others were writers and poets. Their soothingly clear voices cut through the worst of shortwave static.

There were occasional gaffes.

A report from West Africa was being played. "That was so and so reporting from a car," said the newsreader. A pause. "I'm frightfully sorry – that should have been so and so reporting from Accra."

Another time, the reader of the news bulletin didn't turn up. He was traced to the wrong studio and came racing along, legs pumping, lungs on overtime.

"Where the fuck is it?" he shouted as he mistook the broom cupboard for the studio door. *Lilliburlero* – the brassy Irish jig that ushered in every bulletin – was fading away.

With seconds to spare, the newsreader sat down. "This is London," he announced calmly. By the end of the news, he was nearly comatose from lack of breath.

The dimly-lit basement bar, with its fruit machines and fish tanks, played a central role at Bush.

At lunch break on my first day, a jocular, red-faced Burmese man downed a pint of strong Old Peculier ale and talked lovingly of his allotment. A member of the Polish section burst into tears, then went round kissing everybody: three lemons had come up on the fruit machine.

Hardy night shift regulars would slip out for breakfast and beer at one of the pubs permitted to open early for the night workers at Smithfield meat market.

Falling asleep on the way home was a frequent occurrence. One editor woke up on the top deck of a bus among a sea of double-deckers in a south London depot. I dozed off on the train back to our then home in Oxford, and woke about 80 miles further west in Hereford.

Legend had it that one editor, a Scot with a cast iron liver, wandered off one evening and was next heard of sitting in the middle of a roundabout outside Lagos airport.

Night shifts had a hospital atmosphere about them – periods of calm and snoozing interspersed with sudden flurries of activity as, somewhere out there, the news erupted.

Some journalists were addicted to nights: one ghostly editor with a yellow nicotine stain running up one cheek – smoking was allowed in the newsroom back then – was rumoured not to have seen the sun for years.

New recruits were tasked with answering night-time nuisance calls. An insomniac butcher on the Isle of Wight would call in to complain about mispronunciations. A woman in north London would launch into lengthy nocturnal harangues about the BBC's coverage of Israel.

Foreign correspondents learned to stay calm, even in the midst of revolutions or bomb blasts.

"The shooting was of such force it caused the wine in my glass to shake," reported the diplomatic correspondent on a trip to Cairo.

Emotional or flowery language was kept to a minimum. Hyperbole was dangerous.

A correspondent in Pakistan was doing a piece live on air during a coup. A deathly hush had fallen over the capital, he reported. "It was so quiet, not even the dogs were barking."

At that moment, his Labrador wandered into the room. "Woof, woof," said the dog to millions listening round the world.

The Mad Monk and the third secret of Fatima
1981

Local events did not feature much at the World Service.

Governments fell, there were economic crises, domestic strikes and scandals, but we were focused on the bigger picture. The bombings, killings and hunger strikes going on in Northern Ireland at the time would rate a mention, but the problems of Cambodia or Iran were judged to be far more important.

Then, one Saturday afternoon, with bored journalists waiting like crows on a roof for a morsel of news to drop, the bells on the line of telex machines rang out and a bizarre and very local story unfolded.

*****

The copy taster – the journalist assigned to monitor all incoming news and dispatches – assumes centre stage. He walks, ever so calmly, to the clattering set of machines, tears off a yard or two scroll of paper, squints, pushes heavily-framed glasses up onto his forehead and takes a long drag on his cigarette, the prelude to a violent coughing fit.

The newsroom waits. Richard Burton doing the Hamlet speech had nothing on this performance. He loosens a shiny, much-stained tie, runs a hand across strands of hair stretched like cello strings across a shiny skull.

"Cor, fuck me," he says. "You're not going to believe this…"

There's been a hijacking. An Aer Lingus plane flying from Dublin to London with 113 passengers and crew on board has been diverted minutes before it was due to land at Heathrow. First reports indicate the hijacker is demanding to be flown to Iran.

"Hey, Kieran," shouts the duty editor across the newsroom. "You're supposed to be Irish – find out what the hell's going on."

From time to time, you have a magical lucky break in journalism. This was one of them.

I ring up Dublin airport and, more by chance than any clever verbal manoeuvring, I'm put through to the control tower.

A man with a thick north Dublin accent picks up the phone. "Some bollocks says he'll set himself and the whole plane a-lie," he says.

In the background, there's the squawk and whistle of radio communications.

"He says he wants to go to Iran. How the hell does he think that plane can get all the way out there? We're dealing with some class of lunatic here, let me tell you."

Laurence Downey was an Australian, a former merchant

19

seaman and professional boxer who, facing fraud charges over a land deal, left his country, a wife and five children, and went to Rome to become a Cistercian monk.

Downey clearly wasn't suited to the cloistered life; before long he was thrown out of the monastery, allegedly for throwing a punch at a superior.

Subsequently, he worked as a tour guide at Fatima, the Catholic shrine in Portugal, and then travelled on to Ireland, where he taught at a language school. He quickly grew disenchanted with what he described as "the land of my ancestors" and took the Aer Lingus flight to London.

Five minutes out from Heathrow, Downey emerged from the plane toilet drenched in what he said was petrol. He had a cigarette lighter in his hand. He also showed a hostess two vials, which he said contained cyanide gas.

Downey said he'd written up a constitution for the new Islamic government in Iran and wanted to go there to present it to the Ayatollahs.

The pilot calmly explained he didn't have enough fuel on board to go to Iran – how about France instead?

Downey, soon to be christened the 'Mad Monk' by the media, agreed to the change of plan, but then, when the plane had landed at Le Touquet on the coast, forgot about the Ayatollahs and issued another demand; he wanted the Catholic church to reveal the Third Secret of Fatima.

By this time, the newsroom is in overdrive – and a little confused. While the World Service had experts on politics in Botswana and could rustle up a team of analysts to discuss the economic outlook in Schleswig-Holstein, its knowledge of Fatima and the third secret was limited. I was asked to do some research.

In 1917, the Virgin Mary is said to have appeared before three shepherd children at Fatima, about 90 miles north of Lisbon. She made three prophecies. Two were disclosed by the Vatican in the 1940s – one was said to involve a vision of hell, the other to prophesy the start of the World War II.

At the time of the hijacking, the third secret had not been revealed. The story was that when, in 1960, Pope John XXIII opened a letter disclosing the secret, he had collapsed in horror; henceforth, Rome went silent on the matter.

After a few hours of negotiations, during which Downey handed over a 3,000-word screed on his thoughts on the Fatima question, French special forces stormed the plane.

No one was injured. The petrol Downey was doused in turned out to be water and the cyanide vials contained nothing more harmful than a mix of vodka and lemonade. He was hauled off to prison.

The newsroom relaxed and quickly moved on to other events. But the story wasn't quite dead. Later that evening, there's a call from the BBC's Today radio programme. They're intrigued by the Fatima business. Did I know anyone who could talk with authority on the subject?

As it happened, I did – and he was in England. And so a story hatched another story.

David was the alcoholic son of an alcoholic Welsh doctor. A modest but highly-learned man, with a passion for fly fishing, David read classics at Oxford, taught himself French and Arabic, and then wandered into journalism, spending a considerable amount of time in Beirut in the early 1960s. One of his journalist colleagues – and drinking buddies – was Kim Philby, the MI6 agent and Soviet spy.

While in Lebanon, David met and married Helen, a high-cheekboned White Russian who, along with her mother, had escaped the Soviet Union via Iran.

David was offered a job on a newspaper in Hong Kong, so he, Helen and her mother – who spoke no English and communicated with David in a formal form of French – made the journey out east. When I first met him he was working as a Hong Kong government spokesman – the newspaper post having come to nothing – and I was doing shifts at a local radio station.

Over long, rather boozy lunches, David would describe the merits of this or that trout stream in far off Wales and, with the aid of paper napkins and bits of tablecloth thread, demonstrate his skills as a fly maker.

Helen always had an appetite for the dramatic. "David," she would say loudly across the dinner table, "has nine diseases, three of them incurable. And he must not eat so much. I cannot stand that great weight on top of me."

At some time in what was a fairly tumultuous marriage, both David and Helen joined a Javanese spiritual group. Its beliefs seemed vague, but somewhere – alongside talk of the group searching for a magic mountain full of opals – there was mention of the group being privy to the mystery of Fatima and its third secret.

Fast forward a few years. David's marriage has ended. Bizarrely, as part of the divorce settlement, he agreed to look after Helen's mother. David and mother-in-law returned to England to live in a basement flat in Exmouth, Devon – he to go fishing, she to read Gogol.

When the hijack took place, David was in London, along with Joxer, his excitable mongrel dog from China. David at first hesitated about being interviewed on Fatima and its secret.

"They might not like what they hear," he says. "The third secret, according to the people I know in Java, is all to do with Islam taking over the world. It might be seen as being offensive or provocative."

Eventually, after a few persuasive drinks, the journalist in David prevails; he is to go to the BBC to record an interview later that evening.

But listeners were never enlightened about Fatima.

To bolster himself before broadcasting, David had a few more drinks in a pub. By the time he presented himself for interview, he was so incoherent he could hardly speak his own name. He also insisted that Joxer be brought into the studio. In the end, both man and dog were evicted from the BBC by security staff.

Mary tells the punters where to go
Soho, 1981

Halfway through my stint at the BBC, we bought our first house – in Oxford.

I was saved from daily commuting by a friend who offered me a mattress on the floor of her flat in Meard Street, an alleyway 200 yards long between Wardour and Dean Streets in the heart of Soho.

The accommodation was hard on the back, but it was only a short walk, up through Covent Garden, to Bush House. And it provided an opportunity to live right at the heart of cosmopolitan, Bohemian London life. There was always plenty going on.

*****

Every day at 5pm, she emerges from behind the black Georgian front door of her ground floor flat, a chubby, fawn-coloured Labrador waddling behind her.

Meard Street Mary – she is aged anywhere between 50 and 80 – has a scarf tied tightly round her towering mop of black hair, thick glasses and a heavily-powdered face. A rolled cigarette dangles like a misplaced earring from her lower lip.

Woman and dog shuffle off, both with a walk that moves forwards and sideways at the same

23

time, two boats in a bobbing sea. Thirty minutes later, they're back.

Mary lifts the sash and leans out of her front window. A sharp "Come 'ere you", and the dog jumps up, resting its paws on the ledge beside her.

Punters stroll by. "Fuck off, fuck off, fuck off," shouts Mary, turning her head to follow each one who passes. The Labrador follows suit, giving out a series of sharp barks.

Newcomers are shocked, regulars smile. Some raise a hand in greeting.

After 15 minutes, the show ends. The dog gives one last chorus of barks. Mary throws her cigarette on to the street and pulls the window down with a bang. The first phase of the evening's entertainment is over.

Our flat, at No 2 Meard Street, just opposite Mary, has its oddities. One of the conditions of tenancy is that the inhabitants are supposed to be working on a film adaptation of *The Odyssey*, but no one is particularly bothered. Homer can wait.

Modern Soho covers about 50 acres, stretching from Leicester Square in the south to Oxford Street in the north, Charing Cross Road in the east to Regent Street in the west. At one time, it was woodlands: the word Soho derives from an ancient hunting call. But ever since it was settled in the 17th century, it's had a reputation for behaviour ranging from the roguish to the rude.

It's always been an area set apart from the rest of London. Soho is the oldest immigrant sector of the city; Greek traders and the Huguenots, victims of repression in France, were the area's first foreign settlers late in the 17th century.

"Many parts of the parish so greatly abound with French that it is an easy matter for a stranger to imagine himself in France," one essayist wrote in 1739.

Theodore von Neuhoff, King of Corsica, who in the mid-18th century had to give up his kingdom to pay his Soho rent and gambling debts, is buried in St Anne's church (only the tower remains after bombing in World War II).

In the 1860s and 1870s, there was an influx of Germans, Swiss and Italians. A few years later, large numbers of Polish and Russian Jews arrived. Karl Marx, along with his family, lived in a garret in Dean Street.

It was not until the 1960s that the Chinese arrived in force, taking over the area south of Shaftesbury Avenue and creating Chinatown.

Odd characters are drawn to the area. The man with silver locks and an upright military bearing at the bar of the Dog and Duck pub tells stories of his life as a paratrooper, dropped behind enemy lines in various skirmishes.

Two days later, heeling and toeing his empty glass on the bar in The French House on Dean Street, he's in the navy.

"Are you offering a drink, commander? So kind. One's ship has left port and all that. Most welcome.

"You know how it is, a long squall with rations low and running out of money. And one does not, or neglects to, pay the rent. Best thing to do in the circumstances is to dive, commander. Dive."

He bends down, extracting a five pound note from a sock. "Cannot be too careful. All very hush-hush, you understand."

The French House is a regular haunt. I once took an old friend from Hong Kong there, and she was shocked to recognise the barman. The last time they'd met he was on the girls' hockey team at school.

A puffy faced ex-boxer and his striptease artiste girlfriend, who smokes aromatic Balkan Sobranie cigarettes through thickly-rouged lips, are a fixture at the bar.

"Tires me out, she does," he says proudly. "And you should see her IQ. Bloody amazing it is."

Built in the early years of the 18th century, the Georgian town houses on Meard Street stand like soldiers on parade – in need of a little spit and polish, but still elegant and proud.

One spring morning, a group of vagrant lads are sunning themselves on the pavement below. After a night on the cardboard, warmth is starting to penetrate damp bones. Cans of Special Brew lager are passed round.

"Excuish me, sir."

The slurred accent is Scottish. He has a head of ginger curls and an unruly brush of beard. There is beer foam across the hair on his upper lip.

"Do you know, sir, but is it true that the Pope is dead?"

Though I'm not up on the latest news, it seems the pontiff is alive and kicking, I say.

The McTaggart of the McTaggarts slaps his thigh. By now, a couple of other early morning walkers have stopped to look on – a statuesque Indian girl dressed in legal black, and a road sweeper glad of a bit of diversion.

"Oh, sir, thank God for that. You see me and the lads here (he jerks a thumb over his shoulder at his happily-nodding band of followers) have not had a wink of sleep all night, worrying about the Pope."

The word 'Pope' receives special emphasis, emerging like a cork from a bottle. The group twitches and jiggles. One of them, in the process of rolling a cigarette with an unsteady hand, guffaws. Then, like an orchestra tuning up, the rest join in.

By day, Meard Street is relatively peaceful. Two brothers, who work as animators for cartoon films, quietly labour away upstairs. In the window directly opposite, a tailor sits cross-legged at his sewing machine. His work never stops: he seems to have been sewing the same light blue suit for months.

Royalty Mansions, just down the street, was built in 1908 as flats for tailors. Now our man opposite is the last stitcher on the street.

A little further down, there's a steady, gentle tapping from the man who fashions shoe trees – he gives us offcuts for the fire. Once he presented us with a perfectly-formed foot: we waited for a very cold night before burning it.

A small cafe does a regular, if modest, trade. There's a roll of drums from the Intrepid Fox, the rock pub just down the alley on the corner of Wardour Street.

Below, to the right, is a pornography shop. Its Maltese proprietor stands in the doorway, head framed by a handwritten sign advertising 'Adult rubber wear'. From above, all that's visible is a pot belly, a large, pock-marked nose, and a curl of cigarette smoke.

The ground floor of our flat used to be a brothel, run under the deceptively high-class name of the Haymarket Club. It's now been reborn as the Golden Girl Club, a transvestite haunt staffed by a rota of not very convincing girls, all of whom have deep Geordie accents.

The 'girls' – there are five or six of them – do a week on, a week off, catching the train up and down to Newcastle.

In the centre of Meard Street is a phone box. It's been out of order for years, but still has its uses. "Indulge your fantasies," says a card from Nicola. "Tea and cake and much, much more," promises homely Irish Lill. "Every fetish fulfilled," boasts Natalie.

Lust and lasciviousness began colonising Soho's streets late in the 1950s.

The Windmill Theatre, in Great Windmill Street, staged Britain's first nude show. The regulations insisted that the girls stand completely still, like Roman statues.

Performances were continuous. One attendant had the job of tightening the seats worked loose as keen theatre-goers, anxious for a better view, leap-frogged into vacated seats nearer the front. Binoculars were not allowed.

"One fella came in wearing the thickest glasses you've ever seen," says one of the old ushers. "Tripped up in the foyer and broke his arm."

Meard Street comes wide awake as the sun goes down and Mary has shouted her final "Fuck off" of the day.

The wooden shutters on one of the windows in the Golden

Girl Club are opened. A long-haired figure in flaming red perches on the sill behind a curtain of chicken netting, puckering lips, making various suggestions to passers by.

The bar staff arrive at Gossips, the dance club on the corner. Bigger, the large, black and ever-so-gentle club bouncer, takes up position. Up above, laughter is echoing out from the Comedy Club.

Occupants of Meard Street have had a wide variety of occupations – musicians, composers, artists. There was always a risqué air about the place.

In the late 1700s, a woman called Elizabeth Flint – described by the local authorities as "a slut, a drunkard and occasional whore and thief" – lived next door to us at No. 2.

Two of Meard Street's houses were once home to what was called a female penitent asylum.

John Meard, who built most of the street, was a noted craftsman who worked with Christopher Wren on St Paul's Cathedral. But he was also a bit of a lad, often in trouble with the law over non-payment of rates and taxes.

The Golden Girl Club carries on the street's dodgy reputation. It insists it's not a brothel. Rather, say the girls, it's a gentleman's club – offering undisclosed services, along with expensive glasses of coloured fizzy water masquerading as pink Champagne.

One evening, a party of Liverpool football supporters in London for a match weave their way into Meard Street.

The figure dressed in red is tempting.

"Cor, look at this," says a breathless voice. "Let's go in here."

Minutes later, a shocked voice echoes along the street.

"Hey lads, you wouldn't believe it – this one's got a prick between its legs."

Katie is a regular hostess at the Golden Girl.

"All right, pet?" she'll ask as I arrive from a night shift, planting a big, slobbering kiss on my cheek, bristles poking through her thick makeup. Katie is a diligent cleaner, always shoving her Hoover about, cleaning up after the night before.

"I've always been house proud," she says. "You should see the shine on my brass back home."

Outside, the council cleaners connect their hoses to the fire hydrant. The wet flagstones shine in the early morning light.

Mary's dog barks. Another Meard Street day begins.

Postscript

The last BBC World Service radio bulletin from Bush House was broadcast at noon on July 12th, 2012.

The studios and all the broadcasting kit – along with the fish tanks in the basement bar – were put up for auction as journalists, language experts, producers and technicians moved to a new home at the BBC's revamped London HQ at Broadcasting House.

The World Service had been at Bush House – built by an American industrialist between the wars and owned in later years by a Japanese company specialising in the manufacturer of fertilizers – since 1941.

Many of the eccentrics who once haunted the corridors of Bush had long left the premises. Government budget cuts sounded the death knell for several language services.

Lilliburlero, the Bush theme tune familiar for years to millions round the world, has been tossed aside.

But stand beneath the portico in Aldwych of an evening and you just might catch the tumpty-tum of the old tune, followed by the pips and a mahogany voice announcing "This is London..."

Passengers and crew aboard the hijacked Aer Lingus plane flew back to a heroes' welcome in Dublin. Unperturbed, some then climbed on another flight to London, their original destination.

The hijacker, 'Mad Monk' Downey, served 16 months of a five-year jail sentence in France before being deported back to Australia.

The Third Secret of Fatima was eventually made known by

the Vatican in 2000; it spoke of a vision of a 'bishop in white' being shot by soldiers firing bullets and arrows.

In 1981, a Turk of Bulgarian origin, Mehmet Al Ağca, attempted to assassinate Pope John Paul in St. Peter's Square in Rome.

The shooting happened on May 13th, only a few days after the Aer Lingus hijack and on the 64th anniversary of the original Fatima vision. Many, including the Pope himself, said the attack was the fulfillment of the vision contained in the third secret.

John Paul, who had four bullets fired into him, never fully recovered from the shooting. Ağca was caught and sentenced to life in prison, but pardoned at the request of the Pope and deported back to Turkey, where he went to jail for various other crimes. He was released in 2010.

While in prison, Ağca is said to have developed an obsession with Fatima and its third secret.

David, the journalist, fisherman and Fatima expert, eventually became a devoted member of Alcoholics Anonymous. His aged former mother-in-law went into a home for White Russians in London, where her daughter Helen – David's former wife – later joined her.

David married again and, after a spell living on the south coast of England, returned to the Far East, settling in the former Portuguese territory of Macau.

One Sunday afternoon, David told his wife he was going for a walk. He never returned. Despite an extensive search, no trace was ever found of him.

Driving past a remote trout stream in Wales or Ireland, I sometimes glimpse a faraway figure casting a line. There's the temptation to stop the car.

"Go on," I'd say to the fisherman. "Tell me all about the Third Secret of Fatima."

The gentrification merchants have moved in to Soho and

these days Meard Street has a heavy smell of respectability about it.

The Golden Girl Club has been transformed into a polished office, all leather sofas and palms in pots. Katie, along with her Hoover, has probably returned to Newcastle.

The shoe tree man, tailor and cartoonists have all gone. The Maltese pornography shop is now an ever-so-discrete clothing shop, with no prices on display.

The Intrepid Fox pub has slunk away, replaced by a burger bar. At the other end of the street, Gossips and the Comedy Club have closed, and Bigger the bouncer smiles no more.

Meard Street Mary's ground floor flat has been turned into luxury accommodation: the price of a one-bedroom apartment in the area now starts at £1 million.

The pavement phone box has vanished, its promises of silk sheets and exotic canoodlings transferred to the loneliness of the internet.

These days there are more hard hats and high-viz jackets about in Soho than sequins and fishnet stockings. The building where Karl Marx lived is now home to an upmarket restaurant.

The bivouacs of pop-up food stalls have replaced the bustle and shouting of fruit and veg sellers in Berwick Street market.

A few of the old landmarks remain: The French House and the Dog and Duck pub are still there, keeping the developers at bay. Bar Italia, home to the best coffee in London, hangs on.

After we left the flat – the film script of *The Odyssey* still unwritten – an artist, Sebastian Horsley, moved in across the street.

A self-confessed dandy, Horsley was perhaps the last of Meard Street's eccentrics and bohemians. He revelled in the company of prostitutes and once had himself crucified in the Philippines as part of a performance art project.

He died, aged 47, at his flat in Meard Street in 2010, apparently of a drug overdose. Days before his death, he was interviewed by *The Independent*.

"Ten years ago, on a good night here, you could get your throat cut," he said. "The air used to be clean and the sex used to be dirty. Now it's the other way round. Soho has lost its heart. Now the rest of the body shall wither and die."

CHAPTER 3

New York – Dozing at the UN

A pen for Mrs Marcos • The Assembly nosepicker
Tears flow for Brezhnev • Columbus gets the boot from Brendan

After four years in London, life had become a bit humdrum. At the BBC, there didn't seem much chance of a job on a foreign assignment, only years of day and night shifts stretching ahead.

I applied for a job as a press office at the UN, covering a three-month General Assembly session in New York.

Some questioned the move: one BBC editor went so far as to lay a paternal hand on my shoulder. He talked of pensions and security. Out on the Strand, yellow lights flickered through a midnight drizzle. "You'll find it's cold out on the street," he said.

But the thought of an autumn in New York was hard to resist.

Words matter
UN, New York, 1982

The man from Pakistan's UN delegation is unhappy. "This is outright prejudice of the worst sort." Eyes bulge, arms flail about.

A waistcoat button dislodges itself, rolling across the floor.

"I have counted what your press man wrote down. The summary of the speech made by India was given 523 words, whereas the speech of my ambassador was only granted 395 words."

The pages of the two speeches are slammed down, calculations scribbled in the margins. I bend down to retrieve his button.

"This one" – a quivering finger is pointed at me – "is clearly not being even-handed. I suggest he takes up other duties."

He grabs his button, turns on his patent leather shoes and exits.

The chief of the UN press team, an Australian who, somewhere between leaving Wollongong and arriving in Manhattan, had replaced his native twang with a mid-Atlantic drawl, calls me in for a word.

"You're not going to last long here if you don't pay attention to the diplomatic niceties," he says, preening his goatee. "People here are very sensitive. Remember to be balanced at all times."

Within a few days of arriving in New York, I manage to rent a small apartment in Greenwich Village from a Japanese official away for a few months.

The September air is crisp, the sky blue. Warm bagels from the deli for breakfast, the hooting of the Staten Island ferry, even the ride on the dilapidated, noisy, dirty subway is the fulfillment of every dream I'd ever had about the city.

The trouble is the work.

In radio news journalism, you're taught to be brief and precise – to leave out everything but the essentials. The work at the UN General Assembly is the reverse of that process. Each speech, no matter how vacuous or illiterate, has to be given equal weight. No favouritism can be shown.

The tedium and routine of endless note-taking is in part relieved by the theatre of it all.

Along with the Secretary-General and his minions, we press

officers sit gazing out onto the massed ranks of the world's nations, listening to speeches as emergencies are declared, wars condemned.

Global leaders – presidents and prime ministers, dictators and merchants of death – brush past the press desk on the way to the podium, nervously fingering their notes.

One of the Gemayel brothers, fresh from the civil war raging in Lebanon and dressed in a suit that shines like chrome, trips over my outstretched legs, narrowly avoiding a nasty collision with the considerable bulk of Mrs Gromyko, wobbling past like an armchair on rollers.

A slim and sashaying Mrs Marcos, in the days before she grew bloated by corruption and power, asks if her husband might borrow a pen.

The UN building is outdated, stuck in the 1950s. The earpieces, important for listening in to speech translations, are plastic devices with sharp edges and enclose the whole ear.

Speeches are punctuated by wild shouts from the floor as delegates, sleepy after nights frittering away their country's GDP on the delights of New York, wake with a start, nearly ripping their ears off.

According to UN ritual, speeches are followed by respectable rounds of applause. Delegates of friendly countries then form a queue to shake the speaker's hand.

I watch as certain delegates, slumber disturbed by the clapping, jump up to join the conga line, only to realise at the last minute that the speaker is from an enemy nation. Much embarrassed disruption of the handshake parade follows.

The US delegates make a point of looking disinterested. The West Africans laugh a lot. The Iraqi delegate – a Saddam Hussein lookalike – tries vainly to flirt with the nearby representative from Italy, all heavy mascara and bright red lipstick.

One afternoon, in the midst of a lengthy speech from East Germany's ambassador detailing his country's achievements in the tractor production sector, a bored delegate from one of the Pacific island states embarks on a prolonged bout of nose-picking, first extracting, then rolling.

It is mesmerising. Will he pocket his findings or perhaps flick it towards a rival delegation? Will there be a diplomatic incident? Could a stray bogey lead to all-out war? My pencil breaks with the tension: looking down, I have failed to record a single word of the speech by the pale and grey-looking German.

There was little time to experience New York. Weekends were a mix of prolonged sleep, brunches, a few drinks, a walk in Central Park.

A fellow press officer, a man from Minsk built like an Intourist hotel, gives me a ticket to Studio 54, the nightclub of choice for local glitterati.

Maybe the venue had lost some its former cachet. All I remember of the evening is a woman telling me she has a hula-hoop in her apartment. She then falls asleep on the bar top.

There were moments of UN drama. The Soviets and their allies went into a lengthy bout of mass weeping on the day the death of Leonid Brezhnev was announced.

Over the following days, delegates from Moscow – dressed in bag-like suits, and with faces as creased as dried prunes – form muttering huddles, speculating on the new Kremlin pecking order.

By the early 1980s, Albania had fallen out with virtually every nation on the planet. Its delegation consists of two middle-aged men dressed in identical teddy boy-type suits and wearing long winklepicker shoes.

For a time, the two were never seen apart, the theory being that each was watching the other. Then comes news of a renewed purge and bloodletting back in Tirana. One of the teddy boys disappears, never to be seen again.

It is not a period when the UN sparkled. Pérez de Cuéllar, the Secretary-General, seems bowed down by the world's troubles. Or maybe he suffered from bad teeth.

The head of protocol, a tall, stick-thin Egyptian with white curly hair, is a class act, always at de Cuéllar's side. Dressed in a perfectly-cut double-breasted dark suit, he doesn't walk but glides along the UN's corridors, a cloud of Levantine spices wafting in his wake, ushering the great and the not-so-good about with the air of a heavenly shepherd.

In the early 1980s, dictatorships were the order of the day in Latin America.

The countries of the continent banded together to urge the UN to put its energy – and funds – into a celebration to mark, in 1992, the 500th anniversary of the arrival of Christopher Columbus on their shores.

The continent's delegates at the UN conformed to a certain cinematic stereotype. The men had heavily-pomaded, swept-back black hair, pencil-thin moustaches, and wore dark glasses at all times. The women, including the wives and associated female family members who had come to New York to spend a few thousand dollars on shopping, were so weighed down with jewellery they could hardly stand.

The speeches in praise of Columbus grow ever more flowery and loquacious. A whole decade of celebrations is called for.

The ambassador of Iceland interrupts proceedings. No doubt, he says, Columbus was an interesting and adventurous man. But what about Leif Erikson, the great Icelandic explorer? Or the intrepid Gudrid Thorbjarnardóttir, whose son Snorri was the first European to be born in America? They had discovered the New World several centuries before Columbus.

The Icelanders chuckle, the Latin Americans fume.

Normal service is resumed as the delegate from Argentina waxes lyrical about Columbus's achievements.

Ireland's representative disturbs the flow. "Yes," he says, "Columbus was a great man." There's a lengthy pause. "But let us not forget – Columbus also ushered in one of the bloodiest periods of colonialism the world has ever seen."

The dark glasses jump to their feet, arms flailing, moustaches glistening with angry sweat.

The podium struggles to restore calm. Ireland proceeds in its own Mark Anthony way. Its soft-voiced representative suggests a decade of Columbus celebrations might be a trifle excessive.

"Maybe a year, or a month, or a week would be adequate," he says. Another lengthy pause while glasses are polished, pages reordered. "Or maybe just a day."

More pandemonium. Pérez de Cuéllar struggles to restore order.

Ireland resumes along its own meandering path. While Columbus undoubtedly knew a thing or two about seafaring, its representative concedes, the Assembly had doubtless heard of St. Brendan the Navigator, the Irish explorer who struck land in the Americas way back in the sixth century?

"In fact, it's said in parts of County Kerry, where Brendan came from, that Columbus called in to ask the way," he adds.

Latin America explodes. In three months at the UN, it was the most exhilarating moment of all.

Postscript

The UN and its debates trundled on without me.

Pérez de Cuéllar, despite his pale looks and a manner that often exuded acute boredom, proved a remarkable stayer, serving 10 years as Secretary-General. Along the way, he helped bring an end to the Iran/Iraq war and presided over the Soviet withdrawal from Afghanistan.

Later on, de Cuéllar did a brief stint as prime minister of Peru. The time at the UN was obviously good for his health. He died in Lima, aged 100, in 2020.

Imelda Marcos never returned my pen. Amin Gemayel, the man in the shiny suit, went on to be president of Lebanon for six chaotic, violence-filled years.

Twenty years after leaving New York, I was interviewing

Albania's Minister of Environment in Tirana. The minister's secretary, a gaunt man with shifty eyes and a wild, thick thatch of grey hair, bustled about.

A memory suddenly emerged of the General Assembly. Was he, I asked, by any chance in New York in the early 1980s?

The minister peered at him. The secretary shifted from one foot to the other. The shoes were still thin and pointed.

"It was nothing," he said. "A different time. Very bad. I do not want to remember."

He gathered up a sheaf of papers and left.

CHAPTER 4:

Indonesia

An excitable monkey • The dangers of pooting
A man out of Conrad • Hand in hand with an amorous orangutan
Transvestites and Champagne corks

The terms were basic: a non-staff post with no retainer or expenses.

I'd returned from New York and was freelancing in London when word went round of a BBC foreign posting – in Indonesia. There would be payment only for stories used. A one-way ticket to Jakarta was supplied, but Gene – then girlfriend, now wife – had to pay her own fare.

BBC stores came up with an interesting range of kit, more Heath Robinson than James Bond. There was a heavy, open-reel tape recorder, an assortment of microphones and cables, and a set of croc clips to link up to the innards of telephones.

Also included was an ingenious cigarette packet-sized apparatus called a mutterbox, which, when connected to a phone line, would amplify sounds and blast the eardrums of anyone daring to listen in.

Telephone connections in Indonesia – mobile phones were still in their infancy back then – were a perennial problem. Lines would regularly go down for hours, sometimes for days.

An excitable gibbon
Jakarta, 1986

It was a big story. There'd been a series of brutal killings: the bodies of a number of young men, strangled by lengths of wire, had been turning up stuffed in storm drains or spread-eagled in rice paddies.

All were said to be opponents of the government of Indonesia's leader, President Suharto. The finger of responsibility pointed to the army – in particular, to an elite unit that acted as the president's palace guard.

The trouble is the phone in the expensive but dilapidated apartment is in one of its truculent moods. The occasional chirp and squeak, but otherwise lifeless.

"No problem," says Betty, the landlady. "My brother is an important man. He has a phone. We will go to his house."

Suharto, the so-called 'Smiling General', had come to power in the aftermath of what is one of the least reported mass killings of the post-World War II era. In the mid-1960s, anywhere between 500,000 and a million people died as the Indonesian army, supported by the US and UK, encouraged the slaughter of anyone vaguely suspected of communist sympathies.

The country – composed of thousands of islands stretching across an area wider than coast-to-coast of the US – was packed full of stories, but journalists had to tread very carefully.

It is night-time. The only transport available is a trishaw. Betty and I squeeze onto the narrow seat, along with the BBC tape recorder. The trishaw man's sinewy legs pump like pistons through Jakarta's dimly-lit streets.

The brother, exceptionally tall for an Indonesian and with a torso that looks as though it's just gone through a weight-training course, greets us warmly. He has good English.

The worrying factor is he's dressed in army combat gear. Not only that, but the flashings on his uniform mark him as a member of the unit allegedly responsible for the recent spate of killings.

Java is one of the most densely-populated islands on Earth. Children of all ages are littered round the brother's house. Grannies sit on mats, sucking on fruits through whistling teeth. An elderly man with a wispy white beard sits on his haunches, slurping down a bowl of noodles.

Silence is demanded for the visitor.

Considerable status is attached in Indonesia to having a phone. Teams of dedicated cleaners tour Jakarta doing nothing but dusting and perfuming telephones.

Like some exotic deity, the brother's phone is mounted on a plinth in one corner of the room. It is dressed in a brocaded, red velvet coat.

A reverse-charge call is made to London.

The BBC phone system has a lot of John Le Carré about it. In the first instance, a correspondent's call is routed through a group of switchboard operators known collectively as 'Traffic'.

Editors – mostly Scots and Australians – harrumph and grump, blithely uninterested in your personal welfare.

The people in Traffic are different, all warm and cuddly, enquiring about your health, supplying bits of juicy gossip from back home.

I read a couple of lines from a script to make sure everything is working satisfactorily. The various news desks around the BBC are alerted.

"Kieran Cooke from Jakarta on line four…"

It's 11am in London. The editor is in a bad mood. The refreshments trolley has arrived. By the time he's listened to me, all the sausage rolls will probably have gone.

I start to read my piece. My mouth goes dry as the killings are mentioned.

"Can we try that again?" asks Traffic.

The piece is almost finished when there's an urgent tapping on my shoulder.

I have a vision of being hauled off to barracks. There will be a minor diplomatic incident, perhaps even a mention in the BBC in-house magazine regretting the disappearance of an energetic, if not always dependable, foreign correspondent.

I turn, ready for summary justice. But the brother is not in arresting mode. Cradled in his arms is his pet baby gibbon. Both army man and gibbon are smiling.

"Kieran," says Traffic. "Are you still there? We need those last paragraphs again."

I return to the script and try to concentrate.

"It's believed the killings were carried out by the president's most trusted group of soldiers…"

There's another shoulder tap. The brother is still all smiles.

"He likes you very much," he says, pointing at the gibbon proudly. The ape, its eyes bulging, is enthusiastically masturbating. It is also making a series of high-pitched sounds, like brothel bed springs.

"There seems to be rather a lot of interference on the line," says Traffic.

The editor has lost patience. "Some of us want to be home by the weekend," he growls. "Are we ever going to finish this piece or what?"

The gibbon's eyes look as though they're about to pop out.

There's an almighty bang of thunder. The lights go out and the phone line goes dead. In the pitch darkness, the gibbon carries on its squeaking.

The next day, I telex the killings story to London. It didn't make much impact. The news cycle had moved on.

Sex in the jungle
Sulawesi, 1985

Although Suharto's military didn't manage to jam BBC radio broadcasts, its censors carefully monitored the foreign press.

When I wrote a story for the *Christian Science Monitor* on the Indonesian military's brutal occupation of East Timor, whole pages were blacked out with a heavy, tar-like substance. The censor must have been having lunch as he worked; grains of rice and fish sauce were stuck to the newspaper's glued surfaces.

Visas were a perennial problem, used as a weapon to control and intimidate foreign journalists. Days would be spent standing in queues, trudging through the bureaucracy.

But there were upsides to life in Indonesia. After a time, I started doubling up for the *Financial Times*. With no mobile phones and a vast expanse of islands to explore, it was easy to wander out of contact. I could disappear for days – as long as there was a story at the end of it, all would be well.

One article involved reporting on an international entomological expedition, supported by units of the British army, at a remote jungle encampment on the island of Sulawesi.

*****

Henry's interest is in small things – to be precise, in observing the genitalia of the parasites of ants.

Each morning, Henry – a tall, rather shambolic-looking Cambridge don – takes up position in a jungle clearing. For hours, he sits on a small bamboo chair staring at the ground.

"The macaque monkeys are so used to having me around they come and throw nuts at me," says Henry, delicately picking a fist-sized beetle off the front of his shirt.

Henry is part of an expedition organised by the UK's Royal Entomological Society aimed at cataloguing some of the thousands of as yet undiscovered insects hopping and crawling around the rainforests in Sulawesi.

The expedition follows in the footsteps of Alfred Russel

44

Wallace, the great explorer and naturalist who sailed the waters of the Indonesian archipelago in the 1850s. For years rather under-rated as a scientist, Wallace is now seen as one of the originators – along with Darwin – of modern evolutionary ideas.

Scientists in World War II-style baggy shorts run about with giant butterfly nets. A professor from Dublin and his wife stare into a clump of reeds, observing their particular speciality – the Sulawesi grasshopper.

It seems there's a great deal of sex about in the insect world.

"We describe much of our work as micro-pornography," says the professor.

His wife holds a large, no doubt puzzled and rather inconvenienced grasshopper between thumb and forefinger.

"For instance, this little blighter has a copulation speed of two and a half seconds. Beat that if you can."

The expedition is a bit of a shock to members of Her Majesty's Forces, who last saw action in the Falklands War and now find themselves providing back-up support to the entomologists.

"They told me not to swat insects biting me but to check with someone first," says Corporal Al, a squat, concrete bollard of a man in charge of food provisions. His working uniform is a pair of well-shined army boots, shorts, and a bra-and-knickers novelty apron.

"There's a dung beetle expert from Finland who gives the lads a map before they go off to do their business in the jungle.

"As soon as they've finished, up pops your man with his stopwatch to time how long it takes the beetles to demolish the you know what," says Al.

"I wouldn't mind, but he brings his beetles back for sorting out on the table before lunch – says they're at their most active and interesting in the mornings."

There've been a few logistical hiccups along the way. Scientific and other equipment was held up in Indonesian customs for more than a month. When the kit finally arrives – packed by

Britain's Ministry of Defence in three shipping containers last used to hold captured Argentinian soldiers in the Falklands – there are more surprises in store.

Several hundred boxes of 'compo rations' have gone missing in transit. Somewhat ironically, insects have eaten their way through a number of mosquito nets. The supplies sent from the UK included a few gross of white combat overalls – ideal for skiing exercises in northern Norway, but not of much use in the tropics.

Local workers who were paid to erect a base camp went off to a funeral and, having drunk quantities of rice wine, neglected the task at hand.

Living is basic. The entomologists and the expedition's army support – a squad of Gurkhas included – all share one long hut, along with a few thousand collected insects.

Reveille is at sun up, and the local river is the wash place for everyone – assorted squaddies, eminent professors with whiter than white skin, a colonel with a whiff of whisky about him.

A don from Exeter explains that his speciality – the aquatic cockroach – always swims upstream. He places a cockroach in a stream – and it promptly scuttles off downstream.

In the evening, we gather for a round-up of the day's activities. A professor from Edinburgh – an expert on wood weevils – explains the art of pooting, one of the key weapons in the entomological armoury. In its most basic form, a pooter is a long glass phial with a little bubble halfway along its length.

Happening on your insect on a blade of grass or a tree trunk, you place, ever so delicately, one end of your pooter over it, inserting the other end in your mouth.

A sharp intake of breath and bingo, you have your beast trapped for closer inspection in the glass phial. By such humble methods some of the great entomological discoveries have been made.

"It's similar to blowing a trumpet, only the process is reversed," says the weevil man.

Pooters vary in size and sophistication. The professor's is a crude but no doubt effective device, made up of a piece of chemistry lab tubing and a small jar that once held confit.

A stick insect enthusiast from Des Moines shows off his motorised pooter. The more traditionally-minded UK scientists are appalled. The US-style pooter is too vulgar by half – it's noisy and vacuums up the jungle floor indiscriminately.

Pooting can be dangerous. Inhale too quickly and you might find an insect descending down your throat and into the lungs. Two Russian enthusiasts – pooting on bat muck in a cave in Borneo – died as a result of inhaling diseased insects.

One of the entomologists on the Sulawesi expedition says he contracted a tree disease through careless pooter use. It happened, he says, not in the tropics but in the cosy confines of London's Richmond Park.

"I was collecting various aphids when I must have breathed in too deeply and sucked up a quantity of tree spores. A few weeks later, I developed a severe chest infection."

Was it Dutch elm disease, I ask?

"No," he says, a concertina-type wheeze rattling his frail frame. "It was Sooty Bark disease. The doctors have advised me to give up pooting."

The nowhere man
Sumatra, 1984

All colonialism is ridiculous in its way.

Picture the Portuguese settlers, in all their Lisbon finery, sweating away at an elaborate get-together at an opera house deep in Amazonia. Or the pale-skinned British in India and Malaya, eaten alive by mosquitoes and poisoning their livers with drink.

But perhaps the most daring and outrageous act of colonial conquest was carried out by the Netherlands, that small country of dykes, clogs and tulips in northern Europe. The Dutch, originally drawn to the East Indies in search of spices, ruled over Indonesia and its more than 14,000 islands for 150 years.

Back in the early 1980s, there were still lingering vestiges of the Dutch colonial times about – along with some who hankered after the old times.

*****

The Grand Hotel in Padang, a small town on the western coast of the island of Sumatra, has seen better days.

Like many similar colonial era establishments strewn like cast-off pith helmets across the Indonesian archipelago, it stands cobwebbed and unloved, a cavernous relic of a bygone age.

The elderly Eurasian lady at the desk speaks English with squelching Dutch intonations, as if her mouth is full of cucumber. She labours over forms and passport details. Colour of eyes? She leans across the desk to take a closer look, crosses out green and inserts hazel instead.

She rings a brass bell for the bag boy. She and I know the bag boy has long gone. But we must play the colonial game. After a suitable time has elapsed, we turn and carry our bags up the dusty wooden staircase.

The bedroom has half doors to let the air circulate. A single light bulb hangs from the high ceiling above two single beds.

We are the only guests, but at night there's plenty of scurrying about. The Grand now doubles as a brothel.

On the way for a midnight pee, I meet a large, garishly made-up woman struggling to do up a truculent corset. She giggles and wobbles off, high heels clacking on teak floors once walked on by colonial administrators and traders from Utrecht and Rotterdam in shorts and long white socks.

Padang is a settlement out of a Conrad novel. A sluggish brown river curls its way towards the sea, discarded boats lie spent on muddy banks.

As evening approaches, youngsters in crisp white shirts, raven black hair blowing in the wind, buzz past on motorbikes.

Muslims, freshly washed and in their sarongs, glide towards the mosque.

From the Chinese cemetery on the hill above the town – placed there for its good *feng shui* – the jagged hills behind are like mythical beasts, their peaks wrapped in cloaks of mist.

Mr Wong uses a long broom to clear clumps of wrinkled dead leaves from a family grave. Large dark freckles dot his hands and face like burned patches on a field. Wisps of hair are drawn sternly back on his egg-shaped head.

"We Chinese must always look after our ancestors, it is our duty." Again, the English has a Dutch slur about it. He stands erect, tall and willowy. The belt round his thin waist is tied tight. His arms hang like curtain chords.

"The peculiar thing is I no longer speak Chinese. After all these years here I have forgotten my own language."

There is something sad and wistful about Mr Wong. As if life has cast him aside, like one of the boats marooned on the river banks down below.

Mr Wong is a *peranakan*, a descendant of migrants who, escaping war, famine and poverty in southern China, moved to Southeast Asia more than two centuries ago.

Settling in what is now Malaysia and Indonesia, the *peranakan* adopted local customs and dress. Some became Muslims. Along the way, they gave birth to what is one of the world's greatest but least known cuisines – a delicate mix of Malay and Chinese dishes, along with the flavours of more ancient Portuguese times.

In Dutch-controlled Indonesia, many *peranakan* were employed as colonial administrators.

"The Dutch were often mean and arrogant, but at least in those times there was a rule of law," says Mr Wong. "If you obeyed the rules, everything was all right."

Mr Wong's large wooden house is a relic of Indonesia's past, its large verandah opening into a dark living room.

Gold-framed, 10-foot-high Viennese mirrors stretch up to

two dusty chandeliers. On the walls are prints of Dutch 18th-century pastoral scenes. In one corner, there's an elaborate Chinese cupboard, inlaid with mother of pearl. In another, there's a piano piled high with books, spines crumbling in the humidity.

Mrs Wong – she has skin that looks as though it has never seen the light of day – serves us cake and jasmine tea in delicate Delph cups. The couple communicate in Dutch.

"Even my father spoke only a little Chinese," says Mr Wong. "We spoke either Indonesian at home or Dutch, the language of our colonial masters." Both he and his wife were educated at schools where Dutch was the medium of teaching.

Mr Wong's Chinese ancestors settled first in Penang on the west coast of the Malay peninsula before making the short hop to Medan in northern Sumatra. Later, they moved south again, to Padang.

The house has the air of a neglected provincial museum.

The Chinese diaspora settled all over Southeast Asia. In some countries, they assimilated. In others, like Indonesia, they remained a race apart, a minority deeply resented for their control over many sectors of the economy.

In the anti-communist coup of the mid-1960s, many thousands of Chinese were killed as mobs ransacked their businesses.

"For generations, my ancestors worked hard and gained respect in the local community," says Mr Wong. "My father ran a Chinese chemist shop so he could afford to give us all a good education: he thought sending us to a Dutch school would increase our chances in the world.

"But when the events of 1965 took place, mobs raided the Chinese-owned shops and set fire to our houses. Yet we persisted, and built it all up again."

Now retired, Mr Wong meets up occasionally with a small group of fellow Chinese for a meal or a coffee in town, but otherwise spends his time tending his extensive collection of orchids in the shaded garden at the back of his house.

"You see how they grow out of little niches in the trees? They are parasites. Most Indonesians view us Chinese in the same way. We are still seen as a race apart. Anytime there's trouble, we're no longer Indonesians; suddenly, we are alien colonisers, like the Dutch."

In a corner of the garden there's a small outbuilding housing an ancestral altar and stern portraits of ancestors.

Mr Wong and his wife – she is his first cousin – had three children. One was killed in a motorbike accident, the other two have settled overseas.

"Years ago, when anti-Chinese feelings were everywhere, the local Chinese clan association decided to burn all the old records of our families, rather than have them fall into the wrong hands. It felt as though we were throwing away our past or smashing our parents' graves.

"We have lost not only our language but our history as well," says Mr Wong, as his wife gathers up the cups and saucers.

"I hold an Indonesian passport, I still call myself Indonesian, but I am a man…" he struggles to find the words and consults his wife in Dutch.

" I am someone in the middle, a nowhere man."

He chuckles, his sparse frame shaking. He holds up a long, thin hand to wave goodbye.

"We live in our own little world here. It is always good to welcome strangers. Please come again."

An orangutan romance
Sumatra, 1986

The orangutan – the majestic ginger-haired great ape now found only on the island of Borneo and in the jungles of Sumatra – is an endangered species, its jungle habitat continually under pressure from logging and the growth of plantations.

In former days, orangutans faced other dangers. Baby apes

were often adopted as pets by Dutch plantation managers. The tradition continued well after Indonesia's independence in 1945.

Concerned that the animals might be in danger of losing their jungle ways, two Swiss zoologists decided in the early 1970s to set up a rehabilitation centre in Sumatra. The aim was to encourage the domesticated, house-loving orangutans to return to their wild ways.

*****

It's all a little unnerving – like going on your first ever date and being flummoxed by an opposite number who is a little over affectionate, a little too bold.

The orangutan – I'm told it's a she – curls her long, very tactile fingers in mine. She fiddles with my ring. Her palm is fleshy and tender, her touch ticklish.

She peers at me with her big brown eyes, then delicately picks an insect from my shirt collar and deposits it between her large teeth, which remind me of my grandfather's dentures. I notice that her orange-coloured beard needs a good comb.

As romances go, it's an interesting start.

The small settlement of Bukit Lawang nestles deep in the rainforest of northern Sumatra and is home to a unique experiment – a rehabilitation centre, not for alcoholics, drug addicts or tired journalists, but for orangutans.

In the old Dutch colonial days in Indonesia, life on the plantation, far away from the nearest town, could be a lonely business. Having an orangutan about the house filled the vacuum of the long evenings. Keeping such a pet was also something of a status symbol – a sign that you'd well and truly adapted to life in the tropics.

The grip on my hand tightens, arm swung about like an out of control pendulum. We're on the move – my date is eager to show me round her patch of jungle.

She's obviously a lady who likes to take charge. There's a tendency to pull: I feel less like a boyfriend, more an elderly relation being dragged impatiently round a shopping mall.

After the Dutch planters left, local managers kept up the orangutan habit.

The problems start when orangutans grow – like humans – from charming babies and children into troublesome teenagers.

What was once a lovable pet rapidly turns into a creature of considerable proportions, consuming alarming amounts of food, gulping down the whisky and gin, delighting in biting into the cigars and, in its playfulness, breaking up the furniture. Maybe it even invites a few friends in when the master's away.

There's also the question of the unpleasant droppings left behind the sofa or beneath the kitchen table. Eventually, the orangutan pet has to be caged.

I'm told my orangutan is 11 years old and heading into full teenagerhood – a bit moody, but a bundle of energy and fun.

She stops by a pile of coconuts. Is she inviting me to eat and drink?

"Go on," she might be saying. "Grab one. Live a little."

There follows a prolonged bout of scratching before we set off again, she with long loping strides and back bent, me stumbling behind.

It's not easy to persuade orangutans to give up their domesticated ways and return to the jungle. No more bacon and eggs – instead it's nuts and berries.

Goodbye to the slug of Bols at sundown and the prepared meals. The cosy pet basket has to go. The orangutan returning to the jungle has to learn how to build a nest high up in the forest canopy and forage for itself.

My companion lets go of my hand. She's found better things to do than hang around with some pink and spotty human. It's feeding time. Her companions are arriving from the forest.

A viewing platform has been set up at Bukit Lawing so visitors can watch the training programme and see how the animals are coping with life in the wild.

"Many who have been released still return for their food," says Awang, a warden at the rehab centre. "They come back at exactly the same time every day – it's as if they are wearing a watch."

The tall trees wave about and rustle. Shapes bounce along high up in the jungle canopy as the apes – there are five of them – nonchalantly lollop from branch to branch before sliding down a large tree trunk like fire fighters down a greasy pole.

There's nothing hurried in their actions. They approach the viewing area and their food with an easy familiarity, like the old guard at the club entering the dining room. It wouldn't be surprising if they had newspapers tucked under their arms.

Bananas and milk are consumed with a certain grace. I almost expect napkins to be unfurled.

A woman from Frankfurt becomes a little alarmed as a baby orangutan pulls at her skirt. "Goodbye Germany, hello jungle," is written on her face.

A Frenchman is having the laces on his yachting shoes pulled by a playful member of the troupe. The smile on the visitor's face fades as the battle becomes more intense. Suddenly the orangutan lets go: the Frenchman tumbles backwards onto an ant heap. The orangutan joins in the laughter.

Wardens say their charges not only have to become used to foraging for food in the jungle and adapting to a new diet, they also have to learn to compete with other animals and camouflage themselves for protection against predators.

Most learn to cope in the wild surprisingly quickly, but some come to grief or have to be caged once more.

There are other hazards. The sound of chainsaws carving out stretches of the jungle is never far away. Poachers steal baby orangutans to be traded on the international market. The rehab centre is under constant financial pressure.

The light is fading. My date has disappeared, probably off clubbing with a youthful companion.

A large orangutan – a Sumatran male can grow to over five

feet tall and weigh in at 200 lbs – has now taken over as the guide of the woman from Frankfurt.

It's as if he's an estate agent showing a client round a house.

"There, that tree and up there, that's the bedroom. All very airy and great views…"

The warden intervenes. Hands are gently disengaged. Both animals and humans seem sad to part. We walk down the jungle path. High above, a group of orangutans swing and jump through the tree tops, their swishing sounds gently fading as they return to the wild.

Transvestites and Champagne corks
Jakarta, 1985

Indonesia was not considered to be high on the global news agenda – perhaps the reason it tended to attract a rather oddball crowd of foreign correspondents.

The Soviets were there in force, stern faced when sober, tearful when drunk. A sad man from the Yugoslav news agency lived in penury.

An Australian correspondent spent most of his time on the beach in Bali, filing the occasional report on arrested drunks and drug traffickers.

Peter, a news agency man, lived in considerable style with servants and a bulging drinks cabinet. Guests at his dinner table included the petite, beautiful figure of Dewi Sukarno, the Japanese-born wife of Sukarno, the former Indonesian president.

Kate Webb, a quietly-spoken New Zealander who had been one of the pioneering women correspondents covering the Vietnam War, was the doyen of the correspondents' corps. In a profession not known for its modesty, Kate was an exception.

In 1971, while on a reporting assignment in Cambodia, she was captured by a unit of the North Vietnamese army and declared dead by the outside world.

Three weeks later, Kate, then aged 28, emerged out of the

jungle. She'd been beaten on the soles of her feet and, years later, still walked with difficulty.

And then there was Jacques, a correspondent for a French news agency. Gregarious, well read, a dabbler in philosophy, he was an all round good egg – and a hopeless journalist.

With a large family and a menagerie of pets, he carried an air of chaos about with him. He could also be depended upon to relate the wrong story, at precisely the wrong moment.

*****

The Canadian chargé d'affaires is desperate.

Joe Clark – a former prime minister, and now Canada's minister of external affairs – is visiting Indonesia and there's little interest, either from the local or international media.

Enticed by the promise of a good lunch, various correspondents are persuaded to troop along to the chargé's house to chat with Clark's advance press man, a young bureaucrat from Ottawa with the unpackaged air of the lesser travelled about him.

Introductions are made, drinks poured.

The chargé's house is set in the midst of what is Jakarta's banshee, or transvestite, district. Local use of the term banshee – or *Banci* in Indonesian – is said to have originated in the 1950s, when the city's transvestites would tout for custom outside hotels where foreigners were staying and, according to visitors, "scream like banshees".

"Is it a problem living here?" asks the correspondent from Dutch radio. The chargé is a man of the world.

"It's occasionally a little embarrassing – the other night we were coming home late and two banshees out for a bit of fun pressed their not inconsiderably sized breasts against the side window of the car."

His wife, in the midst of handing round the canapés, giggles. The man from Ottawa is twisting one leg round the other, a schoolboy caught flicking the pages of a naughty magazine.

The chargé, ever the diplomat, tries to steer the conversation on to safer, less risqué subjects but is interrupted.

Jacques, our French colleague, slumped on the sofa like a spent balloon, suddenly comes to life.

"How do you think they do it?" Jacques is addressing me.

"Pardon? Do what?"

Eyes swivel my way.

"How do they hide – how do you say it, Kieran? – their John Thomas?"

Jacques holds up a rather grimy looking middle finger.

The chargé's wife busily gathers up plates. The Ottawa man's mouth, about to consume a spring roll, hangs open.

"What they do is, they take a piece of string" – here Jacques mimes tying a piece of twine round his finger - "then, on the end, they tie a Champagne cork."

The Reuters correspondent spills his red wine on the white diplomatic carpet.

Jacques is like a TGV train once he's started. I try shaking my head, coughing. Jacques carries on regardless.

"And then," he says, rising from the sofa and tucking one arm between the legs of his severely-creased trousers, "They put eet up the arse and voila, everything is hidden.

"But Kieran, of course – you know all about this."

Jacques then resumes his seat and nods off.

I was not invited to the chargé's house again. And I never did meet Joe Clark.

Postscript

The Suharto regime finally ended in 1998, swallowed up by its own incompetence and corruption. The 'Smiling General' died in 2008, but his family still wields considerable economic and political power.

For unexplained reasons, the Indonesian government decided to grant me no further visa extensions and, after four years, I was gently told to leave the country. Officials from the

Ministry of Information brought presents to a goodbye party.

"We are so sad you are leaving," they said.

The country has changed dramatically since the 1980s. Back then, the population was around 160 million. Now it's 280 million. Jakarta is literally sinking into the sea: the authorities are talking of shutting up shop and building a new capital on the island of Borneo.

The rainforest – such a rich source of study for those entomologists – is fast disappearing across much of the country, replaced by the monotony of palm oil and rubber plantations.

I don't know what happened to the sexually-aroused gibbon, but hopefully he eventually found a suitable mate. And there's been no word from my orangutan, not even a postcard. The Buwit Lawang centre closed some years ago, starved of funds.

We never did return to Padang to see Mr Wong, but I imagine him quietly living through his last years, watering his orchids, sitting in his darkened lounge on a well-worn rattan chair, pouring over what little remains of ancient family records while the termites chomp away at the wooden walls around him.

The journalists all moved on. After more than 40 years reporting on the world's trouble spots, Kate Webb gave up journalism in 2001: the job had changed, she said, and not for the better.

"It's like we're all mosquitoes dancing on the surface of a pond. We have to move so fast that reporting has suffered. It's nowhere near as meticulous as it once was."

Kate died of cancer in 2007, aged 64.

Jacques also opted out of journalism, though his whereabouts are a mystery. Perhaps he went into the Champagne business.

CHAPTER 5:

The Levant

A freckled beauty • The laughing poet
An elegant revolutionary • Sailing with the Patriarch
Massacre at the synagogue • Nik the fixer

She appears out of the dying light of an Athens evening, a vision of loveliness in a long, white silk dress.

It's the night of the Queen's birthday party, or QBP, the highlight of the British diplomatic calendar.

Booted out of Indonesia, I'm based in Athens as correspondent for the BBC. Britain's latest quality newspaper, *The Independent*, has just been launched.

"We're going to be somewhat different," says the new newspaper's assistant editor, sitting on a sofa, still covered in its plastic wrapping. "Just feel this embossed notepaper."

I double up as *The Independent*'s grandly-titled Levant correspondent: the modest payment terms rival those of the BBC.

The air in the embassy garden on this early summer evening is full of the smell of jasmine, pine trees and *nefos* – traffic and industrial fumes.

There are sausages on sticks and flutes of warm Champagne.

"Excuse me, but are you Kieran Cooke?" the woman asks. Her voice is as soft as a slowly-melting Brie cheese.

There'd been a big story. I'd been on the radio a lot and was feeling rather pleased with myself. A modest nod. The power of speech forsakes me.

A delicate line of freckles is etched over the bridge of her nose. The eyes are the colour of the finest, most subtle green jade.

The beauty takes a step back. Looks me up and down.

"Oh really?" she says, her husky tones now less soft French cheese, more month-old Cheddar.

"I was expecting someone far more, far more...how shall I say? Far more..."

She does not hide her disappointment – it's as if she's ordered the poached turbot but been brought a curling kipper instead.

She turns to a balding, oversized gent in a pin-striped suit, with a face like an overcooked ham. He's sweating profusely.

"Darling," says the woman. "This" – she gestures towards me as if I'm some sort of troublesome insect – "is Kieran Cooke."

The baked ham puts on a pair of half glasses.

"Really?" There's a note of incredulity in the voice. A top to bottom inspection is carried out.

"But darling, I was expecting someone far more, you know, someone far more..." His voice drifts off, a mix of disillusionment and contempt.

They about-turn and become lost in the diplomatic scrum.

There's an image in my head of the couple later, readying for bed. Her face is creamed, eyes covered with pieces of cucumber.

"Didn't think much of that Kieran Cooke," he says as he shuffles out of his monogrammed slippers. "I was expecting someone far more, you know...far more...what about you darling?"

She is already asleep.

The island poet
Aegina, 1987

Greece had its ups and downs.

In Indonesia, journalists were careful about asking any contentious questions for fear of being carted off to jail. Life in Athens was very different.

Officials and news people hurl insults at each other. Veins bulge, arms whirl. The Greek passion for the dramatic, cultivated over the centuries, takes getting used to.

Back in the mid-1980s, Athens was a fairly dour place. The economy was in serious trouble. War with Turkey, the old enemy, threatened.

Andreas Papandreou, a former economics professor with socialist leanings and a penchant for air hostesses, was in charge. The place had a heavy, distinctly East European feel about it.

But there were compensations.

Trips to Arachova, near Delphi, where, in winter, the local *kafenion*, or coffee house, would be full of shepherds down from the mountains, their damp jackets steaming with the smell of sheep and goats.

The magic of a winter's night in the mountains of northern Greece, listening to the haunting sound of a *clarino* being played in the valley below.

The screaming swifts silhouetted against a blood-red evening sky over the temple of Poseidon at Sounion.

And then there were the people – irascible, petulant, bloody-minded, kind, warm, and tremendous fun.

*****

The two-storey, terracotta-coloured house has seen better times.

The green paint on the window frames is fading. A bedroom shutter, its hinges rusty, is in danger of falling off. Patches of plaster are missing.

"Daaarling," shrieks Katerina. "How lovely to see you."

Katerina Anghelaki-Rooke is one of Greece's foremost poets.

61

Philosophers from Heidelberg, professors from Oxford, painters from Amsterdam, and the odd journalist – they all beat a path to Katerina's door on the island of Aegina, about an hour's ferry ride from Piraeus.

To one side of the house is a lemon tree, bulging with fruit. A tall pine waves in the breeze. The surrounding land is lined with a standing army of pistachio trees, their white painted trunks like soldiers' gaiters.

Katerina holds court under the shade of an ancient mastic tree, its limbs stretched out like a Greek dancer's arms.

On the table are olives, a lump of white cheese and a bottle of ouzo. There are stories, arguments, jokes.

"Two proud Athenian women meet and discuss their recent holidays. "Where have you been?" says one.

"Oh, I've been taking the waters in Baden-Baden," says the other, nose in the air.

"And where were you?" The first woman doesn't want to be outshone. Methana is a small spa town on the coast of the Peloponnese, just across the bay from Aegina. "Oh, I've been away as well – at a health resort in Methana-Methana," she replies.

Katerina's raucous laughter echoes off the walls while her squat body – one side severely stunted due to a childhood bacterial infection – rocks precariously on its chair. In her embrace, one arm grips tightly, the other, much reduced, strokes like a feather.

The body – its erotic struggles and the battle to overcome its frailties – is central to her work, as in the poem *The Scar*:

Instead of a star, a scar shone over my birth.
The pain my uncongealed body suffered
Pushed me back into the original darkness.
I crawled on nothingness, my tiny fingers
Clutching death like a shiny black toy.
I don't remember how I came to blossom into a wound,
How I learned to find a balance between pus and
    my open eyes...

Katerina describes herself as a person of two worlds. Her father, Yannis Anghelakis, who built the house on Aegina and planted its pistachio orchard, was a lawyer, originally from Asia Minor.

A frayed family photo album is laid on the table. Yannis wears a fez and sports a luxuriant, curling moustache – every inch the Levantine. The page is turned. Katerina's mother, Eleni, was from Patras on the west coast of the Peloponnese, a short distance across the sea from Italy. She's pictured sideways on, dressed in a flowing white robe and framed by classical columns. There is a dreamlike quality about her.

"My father was a creature of the old, dying Ottoman world, but my mother always looked towards Europe. And I'm split down the middle."

The glasses of ouzo are replenished. From inside the house come the strains of *Lilliburlero* heralding the BBC World Service news.

Katerina is married to Rodney Rooke, son of a Liverpool working-class family, who won a Cambridge scholarship to study Greek. He met Katerina while doing research in Greece in the early 1960s and now works as a librarian in Athens.

While Katerina is an extrovert, never happier than in the midst of conversation and friends, Rodney is the opposite – chronically shy and employing every stratagem to avoid company.

The first time I met Rodney he gave a quick nod and ran off to water a line of tomato plants.

Henry, the house mongrel, was asleep on the patio, the hosepipe curled round his neck. Seeing a disaster unfolding, I reached out and gave the pipe a pull, jerking Rodney backwards onto his bottom. After that, we became the best of friends.

Rodney spends his time on Aegina either in the pistachio orchard or crouched at the kitchen table with a bottle of beer, filling in crosswords in month-old British newspapers. He listens to the World Service, one of his arms stretched up, an aerial for the ancient radio.

Neither he nor Katerina are practical people. When Katerina cooks, she talks, drinks – and burns.

I once encountered Rodney changing bedrooms: rather than find a new light bulb, he was hauling his bedding elsewhere in the house.

Katerina's family was, by post-war Greek standards, relatively well off. An only child, Katerina had a Russian governess.

"English conceals more than it reveals," she says. "Russian is different – it was the first language I learned and I'm still in love with it."

The family would split the year between an Athens flat and the house on Aegina.

"Growing up, I lived in two worlds – an organised, structured life in Athens, and then there was the freedom of summers out here on Aegina."

In her poem *Aegina 1*, Katerina describes the joys of those youthful summers.

> *...At daybreak I would spring from bed.*
> *Dragging my nightgown over plants and ditches*
> *I saw the garden as an endless domain,*
> *The hens important personages absorbed in their pecking.*
> *Time in the summer had no meaning,*
> *The field was eternity, the water wheel turned its infinite*
> *   round.*

I dived in the hay, rolled
Between the horse's legs; all joys
Ended at the sea and there new ones began...

We move – minus Rodney – down to the harbour to eat. Aegina is not one of those white and blue carefully-tended, picture postcard islands. There's a bustle and chaos about the place.

The whiff of grilled octopus and *barbounia* – fried red mullet – fills the air.

One of Katerina's early mentors was Nikos Kazantzakis, considered to be one of the giants of modern Greek literature. It was Kazantzakis – a close family friend and Katerina's godfather – who encouraged her to publish her first poems when she was a teenager.

Kazantzakis, author of *Zorba the Greek* and many other novels, was born in Crete.

"Some years back there was a commemoration for him at his grave in Crete," says Katerina. "The press and TV and all sorts of dignitaries and academics from Greece and elsewhere were gathered round.

"We call a native of Crete a 'Creetan'. But a local official was keen to show off his language skills and used the English pronunciation of the word instead.

"Kazantzakis," he said "was a cretin. He was born a cretin and remained a cretin for the rest of his life."

"Darling – you can imagine the reaction. I thought some of those present would die with laughter."

A nearby table of red-faced Dutch tourists stop eating as Katerina guffaws, her hand slapping the table. There's a shout for more drink. Battered, red and gold-coloured aluminium jugs of retsina arrive.

Katerina is not only one of Greece's foremost poets, she's also an accomplished translator: Seamus Heaney, Sylvia Plath, Saul

Bellow and Derek Walcott are among the poets and writers she's translated into Greek. She's particularly proud of a translation of Dylan Thomas's *Under Milk Wood*.

There've also been a series of translations from Russian, including the works of Pushkin, Lermontov and Grossman.

The Athens ferry gives a final, lonesome hoot. The sun is setting over the distant mountains of the Peloponnese. The swifts scream past, doing aerobatics round the white chapel at the end of the harbour wall. Time to return to the city.

"Visit again, darling – don't be a cretin."

The laugh rides on the sea, all the way back to Athens.

Dinner with hand grenades
London, 2010

On the face of it, Katerina Anghelaki-Rooke and Maria Becket are opposites.

While Katerina is all noisy conversation, bright red lipstick and thigh-slapping laughter, Maria – descended from one of Istanbul's leading Greek families – is a study in understated elegance, a woman of salons and fine dining halls rather than bars and boisterous bistros.

Yet both are Levantines, people who flit – like a dial turned on an old wireless – from language to language, from culture to culture.

Each has an alter ego.

Beneath Katerina's often raucous, intensely social exterior lurks a sensitive and at times retiring person, with a deep appreciation of literature and art, and an endless fascination with the world around her.

Beneath Maria's cultivated, cosmopolitan persona there's a courageous political radical, a fighter against injustice, a person tough as marble and full of foxlike cunning. She, like Katerina, enjoys telling stories; she's also full of fun.

One evening, Maria invited me to dine with her in an upmarket London restaurant, just round the corner from her Knightsbridge flat.

*****

Maria reaches across the table for a bread roll, cupping it in her hand.

"This is how I was taught to throw a hand grenade," she says. Her eyes have a mischievous glint to them. She arches her shoulder and, for a moment, takes aim at a passing waiter.

"Unfortunately, when I tried, the grenade went up instead of forwards. My leg was injured. The people in Fatah made me an honorary colonel, but suggested I should stick to propaganda in future."

There is an arch of the eyebrow, followed by an outbreak of girlish giggling.

It is all a little confusing. A spoonful of *zuppa di verze e patate* falls into my lap.

Maria Becket dwells in various, very different worlds. Growing up, she mixed in Athens high society and was sent to the city's best schools.

But life in Greece during and after World War II was not easy, even for the privileged class. Early on, Maria learned the art of resistance; during the German occupation, she carried anti-Nazi leaflets across Athens, hidden in her doll's pram.

Post-war, there was bitter fighting between opposing Greek guerrilla forces.

Nikolaos Chary, Maria's father, was a prominent civil engineer working for the Athens city authorities.

As a civil war between communists and rightwing forces became ever more ferocious and society fell apart, Nikolaos – high on the communists' kill list – witnessed the brutal murder of a couple whose house he was hiding in. The experience scarred him: he later developed paranoid psychosis and committed suicide.

Eventually, Maria married the scion of a ship-owning family and went to London to study for a doctorate in Byzantine history. Soon tiring of the genteel, bourgeois life of the wealthy Greek diaspora, she divorced and married Jim Becket, an American filmmaker. They had two daughters, but Maria was not for settling down.

In the late 1940s, she had a chance meeting with Count Folke Bernadotte, the Swedish diplomat who, during the war, had rescued Jews from the Nazis. The Count was working as a mediator between the various sides in Palestine.

Maria became involved in what was to be a lifelong passion – the battle for Palestinian rights. The subsequent assassination of Count Bernadotte by a Jewish underground group affected her deeply.

"They say I have a talent for organisation – and for conspiracy," says Maria.

"All my life I've fought against injustice. There have been some victories and many setbacks, but I could not have lived any other way."

It is hard to imagine that this dignified lady, a thick wave of white hair arching through her dark, coiffured locks, was involved in smuggling weapons and explosives to resistance groups during the Greek military dictatorship of the late 1960s and 70s.

Together with her husband, Maria accumulated evidence of torture perpetrated by the Greek colonels. She constantly lobbied governments and the UN against recognition of the Athens military junta.

She was also deeply involved in the turbulent events of the time in Cyprus, organising support for her close friend Archbishop Makarios and gathering resistance to the 1974 seizure by Turkey of the northern half of the island.

"Along the way, Yasser Arafat became a good friend. I managed to persuade him to offer Greeks – including myself – weapons training at Fatah camps in Syria.

"But, after the hand grenade incident, Arafat forbade me to touch anything explosive ever again."

Maria chuckles. Her *pasta e fagioli* has gone cold. A waiter is solicitous: she smiles and he's dismissed with a polite brush of the hand.

In later years, at a time when climate change and environmental issues were still low on the international agenda, Maria turned to campaigning against the excessive exploitation and pollution of the world's waters, chartering ships and organising a series of ambitious symposia around the globe.

So far, there've been voyages around the Aegean, the Black Sea and the Baltic, a trip down the Danube, boat journeys along a stretch of the Amazon, down part of the Mississippi and, perhaps most ambitious of all, a sailing in the Arctic and round the coast of Greenland.

Future plans include a boat ride down the Ganges.

"I'm not a particularly religious person, but from the beginning I had the idea of bringing together religious people and scientists to discuss important environmental questions.

"Very quickly, the two groups came to appreciate each other. Having the meetings and lectures on a ship is very important – it means no one can escape."

The symposia are led by His All Holiness Bartholomew, Patriarch of the Orthodox church and leader of the world's 350 million Orthodox Christians.

A sprightly 70-year-old, Bartholomew – nicknamed the 'Green Patriarch' by the media – has trailed his long white beard and pill box hat through the Amazon rainforest and on to Arctic ice floes.

A few lucky journalists accompany proceedings. The atmosphere on board is, at times, a little surreal.

My first voyage was on the Aegean. As we breakfasted travelling up the coast of Croatia, a German nuclear physicist gulped down a plateful of pickled herrings on one side of me while, on the other, a Cardinal expertly decapitated a boiled egg.

Across the table, the Bishop of Birmingham was served coffee by the sister of the former King of Greece, and, over by the fruit salver, an imam from Beirut and rabbi from north London were in deep conversation, munching on slices of pineapple.

It quickly became evident that Maria was not to be trifled with. She is imperious.

On that first trip, the Mayor of Venice – quite sensibly – forbade our giant ship from tying up on the quay adjacent to St Mark's Square.

Maria was not pleased and confronted the Mayor.

"The Pope is coming to the city to meet the Patriarch of the Orthodox Church – how will it look if the meeting is cancelled because you won't allow us to dock?"

The mayor relented. Never mind that the Pope, who was incapacitated, did not turn up in Venice. Never mind that Maria knew of the Pope's non-attendance in advance. She had prevailed. In the evening, we all dined in the courtyard of the Doge's Palace.

Maria networks tirelessly, persuading governments, institutions and millionaires to give funds, and inveigling princes, politicians and assorted celebrities, as well as clerics and scientists, to join her voyages. She is fiercely loyal to her many friends, but woe betide anyone who doubts her ambitions or lets her down.

I helped organise the media for later symposia. The duties were varied.

In the Arctic, I was ordered to locate the whereabouts of Mecca for the benefit of Muslims on board. On the Mississippi, a light plane needed chartering.

At a planning meeting in London, I was sent out to fetch £10,000 in cash from the bank and, on the way, pop into Harrods to purchase underwear for Maria's granddaughter.

Maria's grandfather lived in considerable style in what was then Constantinople, serving as an architect to an Ottoman sultan. There are very few Greeks left in the city now: the Patriarchate is still based there, but its operations are severely restricted by the Turkish authorities.

"The Patriarch is always under pressure – and not only from the Turks; Orthodox everywhere are always backbiting, arguing among themselves." She laughs. "It is truly Byzantine, the whole thing."

The meal is at an end. Maria hands me a bread roll.

"I hope you never have to throw a hand grenade," she says. A giggle, a flash of those big, dark eyes.

Waiters stand aside. No money changes hands. The bill will be attended to later.

A Ladino massacre
Istanbul, September 1986

It's an autumn Saturday morning in Athens. The summer is fading: the early sun no longer stings the eyes.

The phone rings. An excited BBC editor says reports are coming in of an explosion at a synagogue in Istanbul. Details are sketchy, but there's talk of several deaths. The Turkey correspondent has gone AWOL. Can I get on a plane right away?

*****

The narrow, slightly shabby cobbled street is up by the Galata Tower, in one of the oldest parts of Istanbul.

Life seems normal. A group of young girls play a noisy game of hop-scotch. A small boy with a shaven head is trying to hoist a stubborn kite into the clear blue sky. A tea vendor labours past, one arm bangled with sesame-speckled bread rolls, twin shiny brass samovars on his back.

Three soldiers, faces carved out of Anatolian granite, stand smoking outside the Neve Shalom synagogue.

At 9.20 that morning, two bombers, posing as photographers,

entered the Neve Shalom – the name translates as 'oasis of peace' – and shot 22 of the worshippers dead. Later, the bombers pulled the pins from hand grenades tied round their waists and blew themselves into the synagogue ceiling.

The local media have come and gone, the international press has yet to arrive. The soldiers wave me through the synagogue's large metal doors.

Bodies have been removed, but a heavy smell fills the air – it's the odour of the abattoir, cloying and sickly.

Blood is everywhere, spattered in arcs up the walls, congealing in dark ponds on the floor like bruises on a tortured corpse. There are large splashes of it by the doors: the bombers had barricaded themselves in. Those who scrambled to escape were gunned down.

How do you fall in love with a city? I first arrived in Istanbul in the spring of 1967 on a boat from Israel. Slender minarets pierced the evening sky. The domes of the mosques on each side of the Bosphorus looked like brooding giant hermit crabs.

Walking across Galata bridge, the air was full of the smell of frying fish, onions, armpits and spices. Every few yards you'd be waylaid.

"Change money? Change money?"

Hawkers stood by weighing machines scattered along the pavements: it was as if the whole city was preparing to participate in a dieting course, though I never saw anyone actually standing on the scales.

Walking the city's streets and alleyways in those days was like entering the pages of an Eric Ambler novel. Who was that character with the pencil-thin moustache, dressed in the white suit, tying a lace on his two-tone shoes outside the Blue Mosque?

Or what was the tall, blue-eyed woman with jet black hair, cigarette in a long ebony holder, doing by the ruins of an Armenian church?

It was exotic, earthy, sensual – a city to lose yourself in.

The 'Pudding Shop' was where the travellers congregated, some aiming for ashrams in India, some content to have made it as far as Istanbul, some bleary-eyed, going nowhere. Bowls of yoghurt and honey were slurped, joints smoked.

"You know a bus to take me to Aleppo, man?" "Know a good place for selling blood, man?" In those hairy, bangles-and-sandals, Leonard Cohen and Dylan days, everyone was "man".

But here, in this synagogue, amid all the carnage, is a very different Istanbul.

Aaron Angel picks a prayer shawl off the floor.

"Why do such things happen?"

His voice is soft, the English slightly accented. In his navy blazer and dark tie, Aaron has the measured look of a senior civil servant about him. There's no anger, only utter bewilderment.

"My friends are dead yet I am still here."

Heavy-framed glasses are removed, eyes dabbed with a folded white handkerchief. He drapes the prayer shawl over his arms, an offering to the dead.

"We have only just finished painting and decorating our building. It was looking so beautiful – and now this. In one instant, all is changed."

Istanbul's Jewish community has a long and rich history. In 1492, Queen Isabella and King Ferdinand of Spain, having defeated the last Moorish stronghold on the Iberian peninsula, turned on the Jewish community.

Urged on by the Roman Catholic Church, the monarchy railed against the influence of the Jews on the majority Christian population. There were concerns about the community's economic power.

"We order all Jews and Jewesses of whatever age they may be, who live, reside and exist in our said kingdoms and lordships… that by the end of the month of July next of the present year, they depart from all of these our said realms."

The large Sephardic or Iberian Jewish community had lived

in Spain for more than 1,500 years: many of the country's leading teachers, philosophers, physicians and scholars were Jewish.

In the same year that Isabella and Ferdinand issued their edict expelling the Jews, Christopher Columbus set out on his voyage of discovery, a trip that was to lay the foundations of the future wealth of both Spain and Portugal.

Luis de Santángel, a Jewish banker, put up a large part of the money for the Columbus expedition.

The Ottoman Empire, then entering a sustained period of expansion, was quick to capitalise on the plight of the Sephardic Jews, inviting them to organise the finances and bureaucracy of the Empire and run many of its colleges and other institutions.

Thousands migrated eastwards: some settled in the Balkans and in Venice, while others, accepting the Ottoman invitation, moved on to what was then Constantinople. In 1497, the first book to be printed in the city was published in Hebrew.

In time, the Sephardic Jews adopted their own language of Ladino – a potpourri of the Spanish of Cervantes mixed with Portuguese, Italian, Greek, Bulgarian, Turkish and Hebrew.

While the Ottoman Turks ran the government, the Ladino speakers controlled much of the Empire's commercial life. Some became fabulously rich.

Sephardic Jews formed the majority in some cities. At the turn of the 20th century, the *lingua franca* of Thessaloniki – once a major commercial centre of the Ottoman Empire – was Ladino. More than 30 synagogues were dotted round the city, with names redolent of former days, like Aragon, Castille, Toledo and Magrebi.

When the Ottoman world collapsed, a sizeable part of the Empire's Jewish community packed their cases and once again moved on, some to Syria and Palestine, while others went to Egypt or, in the case of the wealthier members of the community, back again to Europe, and particularly to Paris.

The Sephardic Jews who had stayed on in Thessaloniki

suffered a terrible fate when the Germans occupied Greece in World War II. In June 1941, the Rosenberg Commando, named after the Nazi ideologist Alfred Rosenberg, arrived in the city.

Thousands of Jews were rounded up and transported to Auschwitz. Libraries and pieces of liturgical art and manuscripts were crated up and sent to what the Nazis called the Institute for Anti-Semitic Action in Frankfurt.

Only a few of Thessaloniki's Jewish community managed to escape to Turkey.

"We always felt safe here," says Aaron Angel. "We asked for no protection. We were just about to commemorate 500 years since we were expelled from Iberia, and now…"

His words trail off as he looks at the burn marks on the freshly-painted surfaces and the bullet holes running like animal tracks up the white walls.

The next day, there are services for the dead. A full contingent of the international media has arrived. Camera crews battle each other. A woman from Israel TV shouts at mourners to move aside. From a nearby street comes the sound of women wailing.

"No act of violence could have been so insane, so cruel," says the chief rabbi. "Jews are part of the Turkish family. This is our home."

Over the years, I've made many trips to Istanbul: it was a city with plenty of mystery, but it never felt dangerous.

There were walks on a December morning when snow brought a sudden silence, the minarets turned into lighthouses against a white sky, the smell of roast chestnuts filling the cold air.

Or times spent on the back of a ferry across the Bosphorus, brooding Russian tankers within touching distance, eating breakfast in Europe and a mezze lunch on the shores of Asia.

And then there were the lengthy dinners with dodgy diplomats and not very well disguised spies at Rejans, a restaurant run by two elderly white Russian sisters wearing pince-nez. They spoke exquisite French, served terrible food, and excellent lemon vodka.

I stand by a pillar to one side of the *bimah,* the platform from which the Torah scrolls are read.

The bombers were intent on mass slaughter. After shooting the congregation, they tried to set the bodies on fire. They made a good job of destroying themselves: the head of one of the bombers is embedded in the ceiling 40 feet above.

An elderly woman near me collapses in a black-shrouded heap. I bend down to help: there is the smell of camphor and jasmine about her.

There's a pause in the service as officials rush to help.

The woman grabs my arm. She struggles, creaky-limbed, to her feet. "Merci, merci," she whispers, a young girl's smile lighting up a generous, creased face. For a moment, she is my Irish grandmother and I'm the young boy snuggling in her arms.

There are a further two days of frenetic reporting before the news cycle moves on and the international media leave the city.

I stay at the Pera Palace hotel, with its gurgling pipes and brown bath water.

A beautiful Turkish woman, eyes dark brown pools, sits across the table. The man is fussing with his airline ticket. As she looks at him, a tear runs down her olive cheek.

Is it the end of an affair? She turns her head away. A waiter arrives with a plate of eggs.

There, amidst all the hotel's faded grandeur – the mahogany sideboards, dusty chandeliers, chipped crockery and scratched, gold-framed mirrors – I want to cry: for the synagogue dead, the madness of the bombers, the utter pointlessness of it all.

For the missing embrace of my grandmother and, most of all, for the tears of that beautiful woman.

Nik does the business
Athens & Dublin, 1988

There are few people more important in the daily life of a foreign correspondent than a good travel agent.

Need to be in Cairo by breakfast tomorrow or in Sofia by nightfall?

Step forward Nik Demitis, Athens-based travel agent extraordinaire.

Flight overbooked or no rooms at the hotel? No problem. One phone call from Nik and everything will be fixed. He once managed to book me a flight to Belgrade on an airline that everyone else said no longer existed.

After leaving Greece and going on to a new posting in Ireland, I lost contact with Nik for a while.

Then, one wet, grey early October afternoon in Dublin, Greece came calling.

Gene was pregnant. A holiday on the islands would be just the tonic to sustain us through the dark days of an Irish winter. But first there was the problem of making Greek ferry bookings.

*****

The idea was to fly to Athens and then take the overnight boat to Crete. We wanted a cabin for the journey.

The phone line between Dublin and the office of the shipping line in Piraeus is full of squeaks and burps.

The woman at the other end of the phone sounds as though she's munching on a *spanakopita* – a spinach and cheese pastry snack that often forms part of telephone conversations with Greek officialdom.

"You must (munch, munch) to arrive in Piraeus and see a boat."

A few more bites of pastry, a few more incomprehensible remarks, and the line goes dead.

In desperation, I call Nik. He answers immediately.

"Mr Cookie. How are you?"

Nik has an air of 1930s Levantine mystery about him, a man you might happen across in the corner of a Beirut bar or at a card game at a high-class hotel on the *corniche* in Alexandria. He has a limp and walks with the aid of a black cane, topped with a silver roundel.

Aged anywhere between 50 and 80, he has piercing dark eyes, well-oiled, jet black hair and an expensive jewel on one of his long white fingers.

Over the crackly line from Dublin, I explain the ferry problem. Nik tells me to call back in 30 minutes.

Nik's office is a small dark room up a back staircase above a women's luxury underwear shop in Kolonaki, the Athens answer to the King's Road or the Rue de Rivoli. His glass-topped desk is as bare as an ice rink at closing time.

"Mr Cookie? Everything is satisfactory, but you must follow my instructions. You have the pen and paper?

"First you must fly to Athens. Then you will take a taxi to Piraeus. Hello? You understand? Repeat, please."

Nik has a perfectly-accented, though slightly guttural, way of speech. Born in Egypt and schooled in Cyprus, I once asked him how many languages he spoke.

He wasn't sure. Six or seven well, others he could manage in. He said he often dreamed in French, though he preferred to speak Greek or English during his waking hours.

In Dublin, the rain is beating against the tall Georgian office window. On the pavement opposite, a man is fencing with an umbrella turned inside out in the wind.

"Yes, Nik, we go to Piraeus in a taxi."

"Bravo," says Nik. "Then you go to the port and look for the ship 'Minoan Lines'. "Please say this after me."

The umbrella man has given up. He throws his mangled brolly in the gutter, gives the nearby railings a good kick, and goes on his way.

"Then you go into the ship and you look for, how do you say, the man who takes care of the money?"

"The purser?"

"Ah, correct – the purser. You go to him and you say – it is very important you do this exactly."

I'm busy taking notes.

"You say" – there is a dramatic pause here – "Nik sent me."

There seems to be interference on the line. Is that the sound of someone, somewhere between Athens and Dublin, having a laugh?

"Please repeat," says Nik.

I chant the magic phrase – twice. Nik is satisfied and wishes us a safe journey. He brushes aside any suggestion of payment for services rendered.

We follow instructions, find the ship and ascend the gangplank.

Greeks have a saying – *eyine hamos* – to describe a scene or sense of turmoil, mayhem, a muddle. It's a phrase said with pride – the idea is you haven't lived if you haven't been involved in a good old shouting and yelling match.

And so it is on board ship. Arteries are bulging. Spittle is flying. Boxes of goods and piles of luggage are strewn about.

The purser, his peaked cap pushed back on his head, a sweat-stained white shirt stretching its moorings over a protruding belly, is besieged by passengers waving tickets and pieces of paper. There's an issue over cabins and seating.

In the midst of the scrum, a party of Swedish backpackers in brightly-coloured anoraks stands silent, birch trees caught in a storm.

An elderly woman dressed in black is being sick beside me, even before we sail.

A chicken has escaped from its cage, squawking and fluttering about.

I try to catch the purser's attention, raising an arm, waving a hand.

"Excuse me, excuse me." I feel pathetic, a shy boy at the back of the class.

The shouting continues. After a while there's nothing for it but to cast embarrassment aside and barge through the throng. I make a grab for the purser's arm.

"Nik sent me," I shout.

It's as if Poseidon himself has risen from the depths. The purser, who a moment ago looked as though he was about to arrest me for grievous bodily harm, stops his gesticulating and yelling.

"Nik sent you – and you are standing here?"

He sucks in his belly. Trousers are hoisted, the cap is restored to its rightful position. He shepherds us past the vomiting lady and stoical Swedes.

A door is opened onto another world. Prosperous Athenian couples sit on leather armchairs. The men wear blue blazers and suede shoes, the women are in silk dresses and gold-coloured sandals. A waiter glides by with a tray of gin and tonics.

Through the large window a brilliant red sun is going down over the sea. Mozart plays in the background.

Fingers are clicked. A man in crisp whites shows us to our cabin. On the small mahogany ledge above one of the beds is a spray of delicate red tulips, and beside it a card, rimmed in gold.

"Nik sent this," it says.

Postscript

The freckled beauty at the British embassy party in Athens was never sighted again.

For the first time in several years, we went back to Greece in 2019 to visit Katerina, shortly after her 80th birthday.

Her world, once so full of stories and people, was confined to a single monastic cell-like room in Athens: after an often chaotic, intensely-lived life, she seemed content with quietness and solitude.

"I move from my bed to my desk – and then back to the bed. Darling, what more do I need?"

Though illness and passing time had reduced Katerina to the size of a small bird, she still had plenty of sparkle. The generous lips were daubed with bright red lipstick. Her wonderful, dirty laugh bounced off the walls. She continued to write poetry and gave occasional readings.

There would be one last journey to Aegina. A few months after we last saw her, Katerina died of a heart attack. Her funeral was held at the church on the island's waterfront.

The Greek newspapers devoted several pages to a figure who, in the words of the Greek president, had made a great contribution to the country's poetry and spirit.

Katerina had offered hospitality and friendship to so many; she had spent a great deal of time nurturing younger writers. Yet few, besides the locals, attended the service, the Athenian literati notable by their absence. It was a sad, muted send-off for a remarkable person.

Rodney Rooke, Katerina's husband, had died in 2005. Both are buried on Aegina.

Maria Becket has organised her last symposium. She died in 2012, her wealth spent. To help fund the various symposia around the world, she had mortgaged family properties and run up debts.

Maria was occasionally economical with the truth. A family member later said the original version of the hand grenade incident had been sanitised. Maria was shocked though unscathed by the exploding device – but a Fatah trainer lost a hand.

Memorial services for Maria were held in Athens and London. There were tributes from prime ministers and royalty, scientists and leading religious figures.

"Heaven beware!" said one. "Maria is coming."

These days, Istanbul is bursting at the seams. In 1967, the year I first arrived there, the population was a little over two million. It now has more than 15 million inhabitants.

A visitor to what was once the most exotic of cities might be disappointed. There are the same chain stores as in other urban centres. The Pera Palace has been – as the interior designers say

– refurbished: no more brown bath water, and the fusty old bar with its head-splitting Champagne has been revamped.

Sacrilege of sacrilege, there are even two Trump Towers insulting the skyline, dwarfing the domes and minarets.

Yet go up an alleyway, turn left by the shuttered Orthodox church, walk past the door of the local *hamam* and there's still a hint of old mysteries about. Istanbul continues to knock the socks off most cities around the world.

The identity of those who carried out the massacre at the Neve Shalom synagogue is still a mystery. The splattered remains of the bombers left no clues. The attackers had cut the labels off their clothing to hamper investigations.

Some pointed to the Abu Nidal organisation, a Palestinian group behind several terrorist attacks in Europe and elsewhere at the time. Others blamed Libya, Syria or Iran.

Neve Shalom was attacked twice in subsequent years by Turkey-based organisations opposed to the country's ties with Israel. In one of the raids, a car bomb killed 24 people, most of them local Turkish Muslims.

Services are still held at weekends: the synagogue now doubles up as Istanbul's Jewish museum.

The bulk of Istanbul's Sephardic Jewish community – once more than 80,000 strong – has left.

In the 1950s, many went to Israel. Others set up businesses in Cairo and Alexandria, but when their loyalties began to be questioned by the increasingly nationalist regime of Gamal Abdel Nasser, in the wake of the 1956 Suez Crisis, most were forced to move on.

In 2015, after more than five centuries of exile, the Sephardic Jews were invited back home by the Spanish parliament. The Portuguese legislature followed suit.

"After centuries of estrangement, Spain welcomes Sephardic communities to re-encounter their origins, opening forever the doors of their homeland of old," said a decree issued in Madrid.

It was thought up to 100,000 would seek Spanish or Portuguese citizenship. In the event, far fewer opted to apply.

The Sephardic community, long forced to wander, has become used to making homes elsewhere – in Buenos Aires and Caracas, in Los Angeles and New York, or in Paris, London and Rome.

Ladino lives on, with many thousands round the world using a language rich in song, jokes and innuendo. Universities in Israel and the US run Ladino courses. In Spain and Israel, there are radio newscasts in Ladino.

Originally written in Hebrew script, Ladino adopted the Latin alphabet more than half a century ago. *El Amaneser (The Dawn)*, is the world's only Ladino newspaper, published monthly in Istanbul.

André Aciman, an academic and writer born into a Sephardic Jewish family in Alexandria who now teaches in New York, talks in his book, *Out of Egypt*, of how his family elders would always revert to Ladino at times of intimacy and relaxation.

"To them, it was a language of loosened neckties, unbuttoned shirts and overused slippers, a language as intimate, as natural and as necessary as the odour of one's sheets, of one's closets, of one's cooking.

"They returned to it after speaking French, with the gratified relief of left-handed people who, once in private, are no longer forced to do things with their right."

Nik Demitis, the travel agent, has disappeared from view, probably taking the only remaining seat on the last flight to a destination only he knows. I wait for the next Greek ferry journey to shout, once again, "Nik sent me."

When the posting in Greece had ended, Nik booked us a ferry ticket to Italy. For once, his travel arrangements did not go smoothly.

We arrived at the port of Patras – our aged VW Beetle laden down with olive oil, cheese and wine – to be confronted with a hostile customs official.

A computer did not have the required exit permit. It was impossible to proceed without the proper paperwork. We must return to Athens.

A party was going on in the customs hut. I tried arguing with the officials. They offered me a glass of retsina and a spiced sausage, but were adamant. Then the ship's hooter sounded.

"What are you doing here?" shouted the customs men. "Do you want to miss your boat?" Whistles were blown, arms waved. We just made it on board.

A fitting goodbye to the reliable chaos of Greece.

CHAPTER 6

Albania

Communism gets a bold facelift • Secret of a sexy saxophone
Taking the slow train • The six-month monarch

Back in the 1980s, Albania – Greece's immediate neighbour to the north – was forbidden territory, a country the size of Wales with a population of three million locked away from the outside world.

Enver Hoxha, the crusty old tyrant who'd been in power in Albania since the end of World War II, fell out with virtually everybody. He even branded the North Koreans – in their own isolation on the other side of the planet – revisionists and capitalist roaders.

Occasionally, people would escape across the Albanian border into Greece, telling tales of the brutality and privations of life back home. Hoxha died in 1985 and, before too long, the tide of change sweeping across eastern Europe was washing over the walls of secretive Albania.

The economy was on its knees: communism was replaced by a period of rampant capitalism. A government-sponsored Ponzi scheme – a scam that pays existing investors with funds collected from new investors – collapsed and the impoverished masses went on the rampage, destroying infrastructure, including irrigation systems and power stations.

In the early 1990s, more than a quarter of the population left in search of work, many settling in Greece.

I'd always hankered after a trip to Albania, and an opportunity opened up with a short-term job in Tirana, working with a group of young Albanian journalists.

A splash of paint
Tirana, 2003

Edi Rama, the mayor of Tirana, is a great believer in the power of paint. In his two years as boss of the Albanian capital, Rama has transformed what was a dowdy, Stalinist-style city into something out of the pages of a child's colouring book.

Concrete communist-era blocks have red, green and yellow splashed over them. A balcony is painted a psychedelic blue, a window surround is knicker pink. A purple square on a tenement block over there, an orange blob here, a livid green pattern chasing up a wall. There's a street with buildings painted in strict geometric designs; it's nicknamed Mondrian Avenue.

It's all a little eccentric, but a sign of rebirth in a city emerging from decades of dowdiness and uniformity.

"At first, people objected, especially the elderly," says Rama. "Now they're annoyed if their building isn't given a strong, bold colour. It's changed the look of the city and, most importantly, given pride back to the people – and it's all so cheap."

Rama is a painter himself – not of buildings but canvases, once specialising in depicting large female feet.

"It was an obsession – I couldn't get enough of them," he says.

Rama was a child of the latter Hoxha years. Growing up, freedoms taken for granted elsewhere were in short supply. Listening to a foreign radio station? Bang him up for 15 years.

Humming a Beatles song? Throw her in jail for a decade.

Rama had certain privileges back then – his father was one of the official sculptors of the communist regime, charged, among other things, with chipping away at countless statues of the great leader. The art scene was kept under strict control.

"Anything remotely modern – Van Gogh or Picasso – was designated decadent and banned."

Eventually, post-Hoxha, Rama managed to win a scholarship to study abroad. He was painting outsized female toes and soles in Paris in the late 1990s when his father died. Back in Albania for the funeral, a newly-formed government was searching for a minister of culture. Rama dropped into the job.

"Despite the pull of Paris and my painting, I realised I had to stay," he says. "You can't keep turning your back on your own home, however bad things are.

"Our whole history has been a story of humiliation. First there was 500 years of rule by the Ottomans, then 50 years of communism and, for the last decade, transition and near anarchy.

"Nothing will change if Albanians themselves don't have faith in their country and in its future."

After two years as a minister, Rama was elected Mayor of Tirana, and the repainting of the city began. Illegal shops and dwellings, which had sprung up around the capital in the aftermath of the downfall of the Hoxha regime, were demolished. Along the way, the mayor has made enemies – a risky business in a country with more guns than people, and where contract killings and blood feuds are frequent occurrences.

Rama is a tall, heavily-built figure – nicknamed 'The Bear' – and a former star of the Albanian national basketball team. He says that Albanians are reluctant to confront the ghosts of former years – embarrassed to admit the mistakes of the past.

"The Hoxha time was terrible, but it had its comical side," he says. "The censorship system was mad. When it came to books, only the higher-ups, the communist *nomenklatura*, had access to western works.

"Sometimes, so-called subversive works did get through. Walt Whitman's sensuous volume of poetry, *Leaves of Grass*, was a great hit among students.

"It escaped the censors because they thought it was a book on agriculture."

Jazz was considered particularly suspect.

"I was in love with the sound of the saxophone, cowering under the bed sheets to listen to John Coltrane and Sonny Rollins.

"It was like magic to me – yet I'd never seen a saxophone, not even a picture of one. It was like a teenager fantasising about the shape and feel of a woman's body."

There was talk of a saxophone discovered in an old family chest.

"We drew lots as to who would keep guard on the street while the rest of us went up and crammed into a little room in an apartment block.

"The chest had heavy hinges, rusty with age.

"One of us bent down and took out a wedding dress – it was like a body being taken from the ice, rustling and crackling. It must have been stored there for years.

"We inched forward, peering down, and there was the saxophone lying there, all shiny, with those beautiful curves.

"We just stood and stared, afraid to even bend down and touch it. It looked so perfect, a sleeping beauty. Then there was a whistle from the street below and we had to replace everything and run.

"It was the thrill of the first encounter, the rush of a first romance, sad and magical, all at once."

Doing it the slow way
Tirana, Albania 2003

The legacy of Hoxha's rule of more than four decades was difficult to dispel.

The dictator was paranoid, building nearly 200,000 squat, round concrete bunkers to guard against foreign invaders – exactly who would launch an attack was never made clear. In the early 2000s, many of the bunkers still littered the landscape like marauding crabs, slit eyes eerily staring out from behind hay stacks or roadside trees.

Travelling about the country was dangerous. In former times, cars were strictly reserved for party bigwigs; when the communist regime collapsed, there were only about 3,000 cars in the whole country.

Then, suddenly, everyone wanted to drive, regardless of whether or not they'd ever sat behind the wheel. Most roads were little better than rutted tracks: the accident toll went up and up.

There was also a lawlessness problem. Albanians are warm, hospitable people, but back then there was plenty of banditry about. Diplomats recount the story of a Greek embassy official who rather unwisely decided to drive his car from Athens to Tirana. He arrived in the Albanian capital minus his car and wearing only underpants and socks.

I wanted to travel across the country to a town called Pogradec, on the border with Macedonia, a country now – after years of argument over its name with Greece – known as North Macedonia. Rather than risk the roads, I decided to take the train.

*****

The train leaves Tirana station right on time at 12.05 on a steaming hot Balkan afternoon. There's plenty of comforting hooting as we clank and wheeze out of the Albanian capital.

That the train is going in the wrong direction is only a minor problem.

"You realise the train will take seven hours and it's only three hours by car?" said the manager at the hotel.

Stuffing oozes out of the train's seats. The windowpanes are either missing or broken. A sharp whiff of urine fills the air.

Italians built the Tirana-Pogradec line in the 1930s, conveniently laying down the tracks in advance of Mussolini's invasion of the country. Faded black and white pictures of the University of Bologna hang on the carriage walls.

A smartly-dressed inspector takes a pair of scissors from her belt and dissects my ticket to within a millimetre of its life. With a heavily-rouged smile, she hands back the shreds.

At Durres, a port city, a crowd of girls armed with a beach ball and a large inner tube press into the carriage.

"Albanian women dress modestly and very revealing clothes are not usual," says the guidebook, published some years previously.

Either the local dress code has undergone a radical transformation or the author must have had his eyes shut. "Tickle me," says the message across the bottom of one of the girls' skimpy shorts.

We pull into a station by the seaside: the beach is rimmed by garish, Lego-type buildings that look as though they'd topple over with one good push. The girls are replaced by a Roma family, far more modestly dressed. The mother eats her way through a bag of sunflower seeds. A daughter stares, large eyes a startling, translucent blue.

The locomotive is coughing out a trail of black smoke. At last, we are travelling east, heading into the central uplands.

Albania has drawn a succession of British travellers to its shores. Byron, Aubrey Herbert, Edith Durham and Patrick Leigh Fermor all roamed the country, particularly its rugged, mysterious mountains.

Britain has played a not altogether glorious role in Albania's recent history.

During World War II, British special forces were parachuted into the region to help partisans, led by Enver Hoxha, fight the Axis powers. By the early 1950s, Britain had changed sides and was supporting a party of Albanian emigrés returning to overthrow the communist regime.

The expedition was a disaster: Kim Philby, the MI6 operative later revealed as a Soviet spy, had informed Moscow; up to 300 of those who made it on to Albanian soil were either killed or thrown in prison.

Like a nervous tightrope walker, the train slowly negotiates a bridge over a deep gorge. The trans-Albania line has only recently been reopened: in the 1990s, the railway's tracks were ripped up and sold as scrap as people protested against the country's corrupt and hopelessly inept administration.

The air is cooler now. There are neat, cultivated fields.

Factory-made fertilizer or insecticides were unavailable during the Hoxha years. As a result, Albania's agricultural produce is mostly organic. Tomatoes burst with sweetness. Albanian cheese with honey has the taste buds doing somersaults.

Arthur, a local vet keen on practising his English, shares my carriage.

"In the time of Hoxha, it was not allowed for people to own their own animals."

When the *sigurimi* – the security police – came to inspect the farms, people would feed *raki* (the local anise-flavoured spirit) to their pigs to make them sleep so they could be hidden away."

There's pitch-blackness as we rattle through a succession of tunnels. Despite Arthur's chatter and the train's jolting and weaving, I doze off, pitched into a jumbled dream about bunkers and pigs running riot.

I wake to a magical scene. Down below is Lake Ochrid, one of Europe's deepest freshwater lakes; it is the frontier between Albania on one side and Macedonia on the other.

A delicate pink evening sun plays across the lake's still waters. On the far bank, there are large forests. The bell of an orthodox church echoes across the water.

The passengers – there are not many of them – grab their luggage. There's talk of a beauty competition that night in Pogradec.

"It is to select a Miss Lake Ochrid," says Arthur. "These girls are very beautiful, but they do not smile. I do not like girls who do not look happy."

With a final bronchial wheeze, the train stops. It's 7.15pm and we have arrived on time. Or have we? There's no station, not even a platform. It's a big drop between the train and the ground.

A battered yellow Mercedes stands by the tracks.

"You want to go to Tirana?" asks the driver. "Air conditioned car. Only three hours. Very comfortable."

Six months a king
Tirana, 2016

Foreigners have always meddled in the affairs of Albania.

Centuries of Ottoman rule collapsed in the early years of the 20th century. The European powers decided to appoint an Albanian king. The locals were not consulted.

✶✶✶✶✶

Some monarchs are killed, some are pushed off their thrones, and others are forced into exile. But there are few who suffered the humiliation experienced by Prince Wilhelm I of Albania, crowned the country's first king in February 1914.

In 1912, the clouds of war were gathering in Europe. The Great Powers – Austro-Hungary, Britain, France, Russia, Germany and Italy – had sought to avert conflict spreading to the lower Balkans by creating the newly-independent state of Albania.

It was felt by the outsiders that a state could not possibly exist without a king. The powers, under the chairmanship of the British and with no Albanian representation, took various soundings for candidates among Europe's royal households: "Wanted, King of Albania" adverts were placed in the British press. Eventually, a minor German royal, Prince Wilhelm of Wied, was deemed satisfactory.

The 37-year-old prince at first turned down his new posting: he did not want to leave his castle in Germany, and was unsure exactly where Albania was.

In the end, Wilhelm gave in and he, along with his wife and two young children, set off for his faraway kingdom. The Albanians were browbeaten into accepting the incoming monarch.

A king cannot ascend to a throne unless he has suitable staff. Above all, a monarch needs a good right-hand man. It is here that another foreigner, the cavalier figure of Duncan Heaton-Armstrong, enters the picture.

Though born in Austria, Heaton-Armstrong described himself as an Irishman and professional militiaman: he was descended on his father's side from a long line of adventurers who, mostly based in Tipperary, had won and lost vast fortunes over the generations.

In his book *The Six Month Kingdom*, Heaton Armstrong talks breezily of interrupting a shooting expedition in Prussia to apply for the post of private secretary to the new Albanian king.

Fluent in several European languages, the Irishman landed as part of the royal entourage in the Albanian port of Durazzo – now Durres – in March 1914.

At first, things went well for the royal party. It was a polyglot group. The new king and his family, together with Heaton-Armstrong and an English butler, an Arab valet and German footmen, established a palace at Durazzo. The cellars had a supply of excellent Hock and the food was considered more than adequate.

Prince Wilhelm, dressed in immaculate military uniform, complete with elaborate feathered pith helmet, busied himself designing and awarding medals to various local clan chiefs and bigwigs. Heaton-Armstrong decided the Albanian tribal leaders were gentlemen, though many were bloodthirsty-looking, with an allergy to soap and a fondness for chewing mouthfuls of garlic.

He notes Albanian sensitivities towards women, saying locals are very chivalrous, with a man unlikely to murder a husband in front of a wife.

It was not long before blood feuds and fighting between various factions disturbed royal life. The Muslim majority was resentful at having a foreigner – and a Christian at that – thrust upon them. The prince was indecisive and afraid to leave his palace. He also had no understanding of Albanian ways and customs.

The language proved impossible, even for the multilingual Heaton-Armstrong: several Gaelic societies contacted him, insisting that Albanian was of Celtic origin.

Heaton-Armstrong's brother Jack, a monocle-wearing former soldier, was drafted in to help tackle the insurgents and brigands. A rag-tag army of Germans, Italians, Dutch, British and others was involved in some bloody fighting.

The one boat that comprised the Albanian navy – a small steamer chartered from an Austrian shipping company – became stuck on a sandbank.

Enthusiasm for Albania's newly-minted monarchy was short-lived: with war fast approaching, the Great Powers had other matters on their minds.

King Wilhelm and his Albanian court were isolated, funds fast running out, the forces of rebellion moving ever closer to the palace. Displaying considerable *sang-froid*, the English butler complained that the sound of gunfire was interrupting the meals.

In August 1914, Heaton-Armstrong left Albania to accompany the two royal children back to Germany. Despite having papers of safe conduct, he was arrested in Munich, believed to be the first prisoner of World War I. He was subsequently swapped in a prisoner exchange.

King Wilhelm left his Balkan kingdom in early September 1914, his reign having lasted barely six months.

Postscript

Edi Rama spent 11 years as mayor of Tirana, continuing to paint the city in all manner of colours and patterns. In 2013, Rama became prime minister after his Socialist Party came to power in a landslide election victory. He has weathered several crises and scandals and, in early 2022, still headed the government.

Rama also continues to paint – an exhibition of his work was held in New York in 2016.

The Tirana-Pogradec train line closed several years ago, its bridges considered unsafe. The tunnels are now blocked and the tracks overgrown.

King Wilhelm, the six-month monarch, always insisted he would one day take back the Albanian throne. It was not to be: he died in 1945 and is buried in Bucharest.

Carol Victor, Wilhelm's son, inherited the title Prince of Albania, but never laid claim to the Albanian throne. He married Eileen Johnson, an Englishwoman, who took the title Princess of Albania.

Wilhelm was not Albania's last monarch. In the 1920s, Ahmet Bey Zogu, a local clan chief, came to power, appointing himself prime minister and then King Zog.

Zog, who bore a marked resemblance to Charlie Chaplin in *The Great Dictator*, did not last long. While he and his wife Geraldine, a glamorous Hungarian heiress, threw lavish parties and established Tirana as a playground for Europe's glitterati, the rest of the country was mired in poverty.

In 1939, Mussolini, with his grandiose dreams of re-establishing the Roman Empire, invaded. Zog and Geraldine fled, along with a substantial portion of Albania's gold reserves, never to return.

After the war, the communist regime of Enver Hoxha took over. A small group of old comrades still gather each year at the dictator's grave on the outskirts of Tirana.

In early 2020, Nexhmije Hoxha, Enver's widow, died aged 99. A considerable power behind the scenes during her husband's long time in charge, Nexhmije was unrepentant to the last.

"Why should I apologise? My husband was the ideal leader," she said.

Duncan Heaton-Armstrong, the Irish adventurer, survived World War I and went on to run a prisoner of war camp for Italians in Herefordshire during World War II. He died, aged 82, in 1969.

I came across another Albania-Ireland connection during a trip into the mountains of northern Albania, near the border with Montenegro. A group of farmers sat at a café, drinking *raki*. A young man, a relation of one of the farmers, joined in the conversation, speaking English with a marked Irish accent.

It turned out that, some years before, he'd smuggled himself into England in the back of a lorry carrying hemp and hazelnuts. He'd been dropped off early one morning in the town of S.

Across the road he saw an Irish bar. The cellar man had thrown in the towel the previous evening. The Albanian, built of strong farming stock, was put to work: he quickly learned the trade and honed his English, developing an Irish lilt. After several years, he'd managed to acquire residency papers and was now on a trip back home.

"Next time you're in S don't forget to come into the bar," he said. "We serve a great pint."

CHAPTER 7:
Libya

Gadaffi's desert showtime • The leader's bed chamber
Marching orders • A war is lost • Bang goes the Bulgar
A gift for controversy

The woman on the Athens phone line speaks in polished, hushed tones, the voice of the manageress of an exclusive Mayfair club.

"Please bring your passport to the people's bureau to collect your visa as soon as possible. We suggest you travel to Tripoli immediately."

It's the spring of 1986 and President Reagan has launched a bombing raid in retaliation for what the US says are a series of Libyan terrorist attacks, including the bombing of a Berlin nightclub in which two US servicemen were killed.

Muammar Gadaffi, Libya's all-powerful ruler, has decided to invite journalists in.

The Colonel on horseback
Tripoli, 1986

Mustapha is adamant. "You must to get up. It is in the programme. The leader – he is waiting."

It's 2am and we – a small, sleep-dazed group of foreign media – are being shepherded out of our Tripoli hotel and onto a bus with blacked-out windows.

Mustapha, our Libyan minder, looks like a down-at-heel poacher, his chubby face covered in stubble. It wouldn't be surprising if he pulled a dead pheasant out of one of the multiple pockets in his grubby overcoat.

The bus sets off. Gadaffi is out there somewhere. It's cold. My jacket is too thin.

The previous evening, I'm standing outside Tripoli airport with a small overnight bag and a tape recorder, wondering what to do. Fortunately, a crew from the American CNN TV network – with a ton of equipment and supplies that include a mini-fridge and enough food to last a few weeks – arrive at the same time. They insist that I tag along.

We climb into the network's hired 4x4 and drive down the airport highway. Jane, the camerawoman, who's a living embodiment of the American can-do spirit, starts filming.

John, the network's presenter, is in the front seat. He turns to face the camera.

"Just days after the US bombing, we're riding towards Gadaffi's headquarters," he says in his calm, Ivy League tones.

Mohamad, our young Libyan driver, has a somewhat cavalier attitude to life. Tired of dawdling along the dual carriageway, he crosses the central reservation and plunges into the oncoming traffic.

Oblivious to what's going on, John continues. "As you see, on the surface at least, the country is calm."

He turns to see an oil tanker, horns blaring, coming straight at us.

"Holy shit," he shouts and hits the floor. Mohamad sidesteps death at the last moment. Jane continues filming.

Now we're deep in the desert.

Mustapha is asked what's going on. Communication is not his forte.

"It is the programme," he says.

Then, out of the hollow silence, comes a high-pitched whisper that, by degrees, becomes a roar. "Ahh. Wah, wah, waah…" It's a group of women ululating; the sound sweeps in waves across the desert, beautiful but spine-tinglingly eerie. A sudden burst of machine gun fire is let loose, red bullet tracers splitting the night sky.

Gadaffi may be a brutal dictator and a sponsor of international terrorism, but he's also a great showman – and a reporter's dream.

Burning torches dance across the blackness. There's the thud of hooves as tribesman on white horses gallop by, flowing green robes arching behind them. Cecil B. DeMille couldn't have done it better.

A line of cars – all identical Range Rovers – draws up. Gadaffi, dressed in what appears to be a Michelin Man suit, climbs out and is immediately surrounded by his security – a group of machine gun-toting women squeezed into commando-style uniforms.

Nicknamed the 'Amazons' by the western media, but referred to as the Revolutionary Nuns within Libya, they look like a troupe at a fantasy birthday party. Even at this time of night, they're heavily made up; one is adjusting a troublesome false eyelash.

Gadaffi is a chameleon, a specialist in the unexpected. He enters a tent, and emerges as a cross between Lawrence of Arabia and Jimi Hendrix, wrapped in a long white cape etched with gold braiding. A polka dot red and white bandana hides half his face. There's a little green peaked hat perched on his mop of curly, unruly hair.

The leader climbs, none too confidently, onto a frisky horse. There's a hitch as one of the raised heels on Gadaffi's American-style cowboy boots becomes entangled in a stirrup. Then horse and rider canter off; the ululations are replaced by the rumblings of giant machinery.

"Hey, maybe they're tanks," says Jane, cocking a camera over her shoulder.

In ancient times, what is now Libya was one of the breadbaskets of the Roman Empire. Deep below the desert are vast lakes of water. Gadaffi has a multi-billion dollar plan, called the Great Man-Made River Project, to use the water to turn his country green.

Giant bulldozers and fork lift trucks wheel about. The drivers, perched high up on their gargantuan charges, are all Oriental. The water project – it's referred to by Libya's propagandists as the Eighth Wonder of the World – is being handled by a South Korean company.

A bagpipe band, complete with kilts, wheezes into a tune that sounds like *Donald, Where's Your Troosers*. The Colonel's white horse, minus its rider, gallops past.

Along with a wildly-chanting crowd, we're jostled into a large tent. Gadaffi appears on stage. He doesn't speak but walks back and forth, soaking up the frenzied atmosphere. Fists are pumped, bodies bang together. It's all very sweaty.

After a time, like a deflating balloon, the energy is spent. The crowd drifts away and a line of limousines pulls up. The Koreans bow. The leader gives one last wave; he peers at Jane and her camera.

"Wow – what a show," says Jane, eyes bright as desert stars. "Just wait till they see this back in Atlanta."

Gadaffi's house
Tripoli, 1986

Our Libyan minders say the American air raid pulverised civilian neighbourhoods, killing several people. They talk of a bomb falling on one of Gadaffi's houses in Tripoli: the leader was not at home, but Hana, a six-year-old girl adopted by the Gadaffi clan as a baby, was killed as she slept.

*****

There are burn marks on the wall of the nursery. What appear to be the splintered remnants of a cot are scattered about. A large white teddy bear lies on its side, its yellow innards spilling onto the floor.

"Come to see," says the ever-present Mustapha. His voice drops to a whisper, a monk displaying a sacred relic. "It is the bedroom of the leader." The ceiling is half collapsed, pieces of ply and plaster hanging in mid-air. A large, pink-glassed chandelier sits on a plastic chair like an exhausted nightclub dancer. The long-haired purple carpeting is grey with dust. The massive round bed has a shiny, bright yellow cover on it.

One wall is papered with an autumn beech wood scene, all rusty colours and slanting sunlight. Another has snow-covered peaks and green meadows sprinkled with flowers and contented-looking cows; it wouldn't be a surprise if Julie Andrews rose from the rubble and burst into song.

"The Americans kill the leader's baby, it is very bad," says Mustapha. He doesn't look particularly concerned.

The days and nights flow into each other as we become involved in a bizarre 'spot the leader' game. At one point, Gadaffi, dressed in his tribal outfit, goes by standing stock still in the back of an open-roofed, oak-panelled Cadillac, looking like a statue in an Italian church procession.

Two hours later, we catch him in full military regalia, swagger stick under arm, inspecting a line of tanks. Soon after, he's undergone yet another change of garb, dressed in bell-bottom jeans and a pink sports shirt as he sniffs tomatoes at a horticultural research station.

The Amazons are ever-present; two tall, glamorous Ukrainian nurses in high heels follow Gadaffi about in a mobile health centre.

After several hours careering round, I see a chance to grab a few words. Gadaffi is coming out of a mosque and climbing into a racy-looking Lancia.

I poke a microphone through the car window. There's a US aircraft carrier parked off the Libyan coast. Is the Colonel worried about another US raid?

"We don't have time to talk about this now," says the Colonel. His voice is tired and a little reedy, like an out-of tune trumpet. There is an awkward moment as we both struggle to free my microphone, trapped as the car window closes.

And that was it. All the chasing about the desert for that one quote. Hardly a scoop.

Called to parade
Tripoli, 1986

Towards the end of that first trip to Libya, even Jane, the ever-enthusiastic camera woman, has had enough of Mustapha's night-time trysts and the Gadaffi roadshow.

The main body of the journalists' party has gone to cover a military parade. We go on strike and sit in the hotel, eating spaghetti and watching events on TV.

An old military hand once said an army's combat effectiveness could be measured in adverse proportion to the amount of medals and ribbons on display.

Colonel Gadaffi and his fellow officers are dressed like Christmas trees. There is enough braid about to furnish a Victorian boudoir. Chests are ablaze with honours. Peaked hats are shined and plumed.

A tank breaks down in front of the main viewing platform, farting clouds of thick black diesel smoke over the elite. In the stifling heat, the bagpipers manage only a wheezy warble. The make-up on the Revolutionary Nuns is melting.

The Colonel is not happy. He leans across to one of his aides, gesticulating fiercely. Within minutes, a frantic Mustapha is banging on the door.

Gadaffi has noticed our absence. Perhaps he's taken a shine to Jane.

More for the sake of Mustapha's blood pressure than anything else, we load ourselves into waiting jeeps and, along with cameras and tape recorders, arrive at the celebrations.

The soldiers resume their marching. The missiles slide by. The Colonel takes off his shades and smiles for the cameras. Order is restored.

Soccer in the Sahara
Aouzou Strip, 1987

There's been a battle. A jet screams down the runway, flames from its exhaust bursting into the sky. An army helicopter lands nearby, throwing up great balls of tumbleweed and desert dust.

It's my second visit to Libya, and this time – rather than spending time playing hide and seek with Gadaffi – a party of journalists has been flown to a military base in southern Libya, on the country's border with Chad.

*****

One of the minders, dressed in a dapper white outfit more suited for a night at the gaming tables than a battlefield tour, leans over my shoulder.

"Titti noon at spars," he says.

"Pardon?"

"Titti noon. I like very much. My team."

The minder has an anxious, betting shop air about him. He bites a nail and looks round furtively before pulling a crumpled piece of paper from his wallet. It's a ticket for a Tottenham Hotspur v Liverpool game.

Further football talk is drowned out by the clacking tracks of a passing tank, a noise like falling dominoes.

We are at Wadi Doum, an oasis deep in the Sahara and site of one of Libya's biggest military bases.

Libya and Chad, its neighbour to the south, have been fighting for years over ownership of a piece of desert and rocks called the Aouzou Strip, one of the remotest areas on Earth.

There'd been hours of waiting round at a military airport outside Tripoli, followed by a long flight south in a draughty Hercules, the floor space littered with stretchers.

Now we're being shoved up the backside of a Chinook helicopter en route to the battlefield: Colonel Gadaffi's forces are claiming a great victory.

One of our group is out of sorts. Tall and wispy, with a look of the cricket pitch about him, he writes for a trade magazine.

"I was invited to a conference on pipes and pumping stations – I don't know why I've become mixed up in this."

The Aouzou Strip, about 100 miles wide and 500 miles long, is one of those peculiar legacies of the colonial carve-up of Africa.

The French and Italian occupiers of the region, with a little help from the British, used their pencils and rulers to draw arbitrary borders across thousands of miles of desert.

The Strip is believed to contain valuable uranium deposits. Chad claims the area as part of its territory. Libya has other ideas.

Libyan jets had bombed a convoy of Chadian forces. Fighters on the ground had tried to flee.

Three bodies are spread-eagled on the side of a sand dune. Several others lie under an oil tanker, flies creating a funereal buzz. A dead soldier still sits upright at the wheel of a jeep, body bloated in the heat.

I join the pipes and pumps man behind a burned-out truck for a bout of vomiting and retching. Someone says the smell of ripe fruit indicates that the Libyans have been using napalm.

The Tottenham fan intervenes.

"No, no," he says, waving his arms about as if appealing against a penalty decision. "Libya never uses the napalm – it is against the rules."

On the face of it, it's been an unequal contest. The Libyans have Soviet-made jets, helicopters and tanks, and stores packed with bombs and ammunition.

But this is a rare victory for Gadaffi's forces. The opposition is enterprising. In what's become known as the 'Toyota War', the Chadians have been using small convoys of jeeps, mounted with machine guns and rocket launchers, to carry out lightening raids on the Colonel's more cumbersome military.

Libya's tanks, all very fine for charging across the Russian steppe, are not suited to the shifting sands and heat of the desert, their crews frying in the non-air conditioned interiors. There have been a number of humiliating defeats.

I look at a pile of spent armaments, an advert for the international arms trade. There are manufacturers' markings from the US, Czechoslovakia, the Soviet Union, Israel and the UK.

"You must be careful – some of them could be live."

The voice is authoritative, with a distinctly Sandhurst topping to it.

Colonel Mohammed would be at home in any British officers' mess, the sort of chap who might slide a chit book along the bar or pop his carefully-rolled linen serviette – with its silver ring – into the row of pigeon holes by the door.

"This is only the first phase in the battle," he says. Each syllable is as clipped as a military haircut.

"The enemy is cunning, using modern equipment but old tactics, never committing large forces."

The Colonel did his first bout of officer training in East Germany, then Russia. He went to be "finished off" at officers' college in Rawalpindi, Pakistan – Sandhurst in the sun.

He doesn't entirely approve of the circumstances he finds himself in.

"We have the wrong equipment for fighting a war like this," he says, shouting over the sound of the helicopter's rotor blades as we fly back to Wadi Doum.

Two soldiers lie on nearby stretchers, their eyes open, unblinking. One has a badly shattered leg, the other has a bloodied bandage wrapped round his head.

The light is fading fast, the sky turning a brilliant pink.

The dim shadows of tank emplacements are spread across the desert valley below, a fire burning beside each one. It is suddenly bitterly cold. Machine gun fire spits into the sky.

"They are celebrating," says the Colonel. "I tell them they are giving away their positions, but what can you do?"

With an almighty bang, we land back at base. My military companion chuckles, patting me on the knee.

"My friend, the prophet must be smiling on us. This pilot has never flown at night before."

The Bulgarian Quartermaster
Tripoli, 1987

Libya is full of strange encounters.

An Irish friend, a meat trader selling live cattle and sheep and in Tripoli for the first time, was having breakfast when he heard familiar accents at an adjoining table.

"Hello lads – are you in the meat trade as well?" he asked.

There was a pause and cold-bladed stares.

In the early 1970s, and again in the mid-1980s, Libya was one of the IRA's big arms suppliers.

"No, we are not in the meat trade – and what's it to you?" replied one of the men, his Belfast accent as sharp as an abattoir knife.

*****

Wandering into my hotel's dimly-lit basement lounge one afternoon, I trip over a pair of legs. A man in an ill-fitting suit looks up.

"You from Rome? "

The English is heavily accented. The speaker doesn't wait for an answer but casts a suspicious glance round the room. The only other occupant is a large white fish drifting lazily round a tank illuminated by a dim green light.

"I am from Bulgaria." One of his eyelids flutters involuntarily. A bottle of reddish-looking fluid is pulled from inside his jacket. Two small paper cups – they look like medicine pots for distributing pills – are conjured out of a pocket.

Eastern bloc countries have been active in Libya for years, mostly involved in arming and training the country's military.

Cups are drained.

"Good, no?" The liquid – it's Ukrainian chilli vodka – scours the throat.

The man – let's call him Pavel – is an army advisor. There's the chance that this might be a set-up, but Pavel seems too drunk to be play-acting.

He's in love with the desert.

"She is so beautiful." He puts a finger up to his lips. "It is so quiet – and the stars, they are always so clear and bright."

Pavel, it turns out, is a quartermaster, helping set up military supply depots round Libya. There is a Slavic sadness about him. His eyes are watery. The fish has stopped its circuits of the tank. It, too, has a maudlin look.

"I do my job. I make maps, give numbers of where everything is. Then I am asked to go home."

A long pause. Another slurp of vodka. This time he doesn't offer me any.

Two years pass. He returns to find that all the officers he's trained have been replaced in one of Gadaffi's periodic purges of the military.

"My maps, my lists, they have all disappeared. It is a disaster."

Fierce winds blow across the Sahara and the desert landscape is constantly reshaping itself. There's a good chance that many of the arsenals are now buried under heaps of sand.

Pavel, like any army officer worth his stripes, has great pride in his work, but it's all gone to waste. Not only that but his unmarked dumps might result in a calamity of major proportions.

The gelignite and piles of ammunition, left sweating away out in the desert heat, could easily explode.

"Boom, boom," he shouts, his backside lifting off the sofa.

The white fish does a frightened flip.

Doing it by the book
Tripoli, 1986

Mao Tse Tung had his *Little Red Book* of revolutionary sayings. Not to be outdone, Colonel Gadaffi had his *Green Book*, a sort of DIY manual on refashioning society and running a successful dictatorship.

Returning to the hotel one evening, a copy lay on the bedside table, the local substitute for a Gideon Bible. Maybe the script had lost something in translation, but it seemed a little rambling and confused.

"Horsemen who hold the reins of their horses have no seat in the grandstands at the racecourse," it said. There were musings on the economy, the role of women, and then it returned to the race track.

"The grandstand will disappear when no one is there to occupy it."

Alongside the book is another present – an expensive Japanese camera.

Accepting gifts, whether in the form of free trips, nights in hotels, bottles of brandy or of cameras, is a grey area for journalists. On one hand, you don't want to be compromised and be accused of accepting bribes. But neither do you want to cause offence. In the Arab world, the return of gifts is seen as deeply insulting.

A shrill American journalist has a clear opinion on the matter.

"We're not allowed to accept gifts worth more than $25," she says. "You know they're trying to buy us – we must give the cameras back."

A newspaper man from Rome, with a girth more suited to the corner table in a trattoria than bouncing around the deserts of North Africa, is part of the reporting party.

He sits by the hotel swimming pool, using me as his daily news provider.

"I am rather old and tired for this job – just tell me a little of what happened." His bald pate shines in the Tripoli sun. A splendid white regimental moustache is given a twist.

He's heard about the cameras: there's talk of divisions in the journalistic ranks.

"These Americans, they are not like us; they are such children. We Europeans are different people. More realistic, more understanding, more flexible.

"If they don't want their cameras, they can give them to me – I can always find a good home for them."

Postscript

Muammar Gadaffi, self-styled liberator of the Arab world and King of Kings of Africa, met an inglorious end.

In late 2011, as the chaos of civil war unfolded, the Colonel was dragged from his hiding place in a drain near his home city of Sirte, sodomised with a stick, and shot. His body was laid out for viewing in a meat freezer.

Through his more than 40 years in power, Gadaffi was both the perpetrator and victim of international warfare and the dark arts of espionage. For three decades, the Libyan leader was branded a pariah by the West, a terrorist who connived in numerous acts of violence around the world, including the downing of a Pan Am passenger jet over Scotland and supplying the IRA with boatloads of arms.

Yet by 2004, in the wake of the 9/11 bombings, Gadaffi had been welcomed back into the international fold, valued as an important ally in the fight against Al Qaeda and other groups. Tony Blair went to Tripoli and kissed the leader on the cheek.

Western firms won fat contracts in Libya's oil industry. British and US intelligence agencies cosied up to the Libyans, aiding and abetting the return of Gadaffi opponents to Tripoli – to be subjected to various unpleasant welcome home treatments.

Then, when civil war broke out, the West switched sides again. Britain and France launched bombing raids on Gadaffi's forces. As the Libyan regime tottered, Messrs Cameron and Sarkozy went to Benghazi, promising never to abandon Libya – which they promptly did, with dire results.

The Great Man-Made River scheme is still unfinished: the South Korean company involved went bust.

Mystery surrounds the fate of Hana, Gadaffi's adopted daughter, supposedly killed during the 1986 US bombing raid. Some say Hana escaped the bombs and is now practising as a doctor somewhere in Libya. Others say another girl, unrelated to the Gadaffi clan, died.

Mustapha, the ever-present minder, disappeared without trace.

Shortly after our visit to the Aouzou Strip, the Chadians swept into the Wadi Doum base, capturing more than 3,000 Libyan soldiers.

In what must rank as one of the biggest abandonments of military hardware in history, the Libyans left behind at least 200 Soviet T55 tanks, a dozen helicopters and 20 Czech-made fighter jets, along with vast stocks of ammunition and sophisticated radar and communications equipment.

In 1994, the Aouzou Strip was declared to be part of Chad's territory by the International Court of Justice.

The fate of Colonel Mohammed, the desert commander, is unknown. The Bulgarian quartermaster was last seen asleep by the fish tank in the hotel lounge. I lost contact with the CNN crew and Jane; she's probably either shooting a film in the backwaters of Baluchistan or running a yoga retreat in the mountains of Montana.

In return for assistance rendered, my Italian journalist friend later treated me to a slap-up dinner at one of Rome's best restaurants.

I still have my copy of Muammar Gadaffi's *Green Book* – and the camera.

CHAPTER 8:
The Papal trail

Nearly a priest • The Papa talks pidgin • Mass with Fidel and Che
Red socks in Rome • Ordained at last

It could all have been so different. If life had unfurled itself in other ways, there's a good chance I'd be wearing a cardinal's hat by now or, at the very least, have a bishop's crozier propped behind the door.

At the age of nine, I was sent to a boarding school in a dark valley in North Staffordshire. Cotton College was an awful place, run by priests. There was enough caning, bullying and bad food to last several lifetimes.

After all the years, the smell of mince, floor polish and incense lives on. One ear is bigger than the other due to its frequent wrenching by a sadistic maths teacher.

It was either lessons or church. Up at 6.30 for mass – breaking the ice in the washbasins – then hymns at noon and another service in the evenings.

On Sundays, there'd be a treble bill: low mass, a quick breakfast, then high mass followed by a pastoral talk – and

Compline and Benediction added on in the evening.

For me, there was an additional ecclesiastical burden. During my first two months at Cotton, I kept being hauled out of the dormitory extra early for altar boy duties. After a while, I summoned up the courage to ask one of the priests what was going on.

The priest – he smelled of carbolic soap – pulled a red notebook from the top pocket of his cassock.

"Ah," he said, "you're down as possible priestly material."

I stammered, gulped. Surely there must be a mistake?

"No," said the priest, drifting away on squeaking rubber-soled shoes. "Your father put you on the list."

Both my elder brother Brendan and myself had been sent to board at Cotton. Our parents did not act out of malice. They – both from relatively humble backgrounds – were probably seduced by the idea of private education and the opportunities it might offer.

Arthur, our father, was not a staunch Catholic: he had converted in order to marry Rita, our very Irish mother.

"Why did you tell them I might become a priest?" I asked Arthur during the next, once-a-term, parental visit.

We were sitting in the stuffy, rather seedy dining room of a hotel in Stoke-on-Trent. Arthur took a long pull on his glass of Guinness. He was dressed in loud tweeds, his red hair poking out from beneath his peaked cap, looking like a bookie who'd just made a killing against the odds.

Starved for weeks, I was ladling platefuls of food down. He taps my knee, gives a wink.

"Remember, son – always grab a bargain when you see one; they said they'd knock off half the fees if you were put down for the priesthood."

In the end, journalism won out over the clerical life.

Faced with a Latin test, I faked a stomach ache. The doctor diagnosed appendicitis and whisked me off to hospital, where the offending organ – probably wondering what all the fuss was about – was extracted.

The process was painful, but there was also a tremendous sense of relief. There were even grown-ups around who believed in fun. One scrunched up a newspaper and organised a game of football on the ward – Appendix v Haemorrhoids, the former team bent over, the latter holding on to their arses.

It was the end of my schooldays at Cotton, but maybe that early ecclesiastical skirmish did have an effect.

Over the years – whether by design or divine intervention – I covered several religious stories, including a number of papal tours.

The Papa goes native
Papua New Guinea, 1984

The engines of the *Dante Alighieri*, the papal jet, whine to a stop. It's evening at the small airport outside Port Moresby, the capital of Papua New Guinea. Palm trees are silhouetted against a lipstick-red evening sky.

Travel-creased photographers and film crews run down the back steps of the plane, an undignified mass jostling each other for space. Pope John Paul, white cassock swirling in the wind, comes down the front steps, kneels, and kisses the tarmac.

He speaks in pidgin.

"You, me think think, big fellow, he belong Jesus, go, get up…"

Roman Catholicism competes alongside numerous other religions in Papua New Guinea. In former times, some might have seen the arrival of the Pope as a manifestation of the cargo cult, with people believing that outsiders brought not only goods and money but also the chance of moral salvation.

Whatever their beliefs, locals are determined to put on a rousing show for the pontiff. Tribespeople, painted and dressed in multiple colours and wearing elaborate half moon headdresses, dance and chant: "You number one, Jesus man." Drummers bang out a frenzied beat. A bare-chested woman, red and yellow lines running over her heavily-oiled torso, does a vigorous shimmy in her 'arse grass' skirt.

"All bishops belong you fella," says the Pope. "He good fella, belong God..."

A 21-gun salute goes off, each volley greeted by giggles and dancing. The smoke from the gun envelops the papal entourage and local dignitaries. There's much coughing – and more laughter.

A choir sings the Polish hymn *Black Madonna*. It is discordant, ragged and achingly beautiful. John Paul extracts a large white handkerchief from a cassock sleeve like a rabbit from a hat. Papal eyes are dabbed.

I go into the small airport building to splice and sort out yards of tangled tape. By the time I emerge, the whole show has moved on, the crowds have dispersed. There's no sign of a taxi.

The narrow, potholed road goes through a coconut plantation. A woman with a water pitcher on her head walks in front, her body swaying in time with the waving trees.

From behind, there's a polite beep of a horn.

The white popemobile approaches, the Pope standing in the back grasping a handrail, a Punch and Judy puppet. For a magical moment, there are no motorcycle outriders, no police cars: it's like being alone in a theatre, watching actors move slowly across the stage.

The popemobile comes to a stop. A woman appears out of the roadside bushes, baby in arms. John Paul bends, kisses the baby's head, blesses it.

My eye level is in line with the pontiff's feet. There's no sign of delicate red leather slippers: instead, there is a cumbersome-looking pair of scuffed workers' boots, the lace of one undone.

I raise my head. The Pope's hands are large, the knuckles calloused. In his youth in Poland, Karol Wojtyla played goalie in the local football team. He has an uncle's open face – someone you'd talk to about girlfriend troubles or turn to after an argument with your dad.

Our eyes meet. There's a matey, looking-up-to-heaven moment. It's as if we're Laurel and Hardy: "Another fine mess you've got me into," is the message.

Do I offer the Pope the microphone and ask his opinion on the state of the world? Or should I fall to my knees and ask forgiveness for a whole catalogue of sins? For some reason, I find myself giving the Vicar of Christ a thumbs up.

Another toot from the popemobile. The pontiff smiles, shrugs his shoulders and moves off down the rutted road, his billowing robes blowing like a ship's sail in an unsettled sea.

✶✶✶✶✶

Popes have come in all manner of guises, some saints, some scoundrels.

Pope Damascus, elected to the throne of St Peter at the end of the 4th century, was a bit of a lad, nicknamed *matronarum auriscalpius*, or the ladies' ear tickler, due to his habit of frequenting the houses of rich widows and heiresses.

He was also a dab hand at composing poetic verses on the subject of virginity.

Popes have been poisoned, strangled and suffocated. When Pope Formosus died in 896, he did not rest peacefully in his grave. His successor, Stephen VI, clearly a man with a grudge, had his predecessor's corpse dug up and put on trial.

The so-called 'Cadaver Synod' found Formosus guilty of various crimes, his body thereafter tossed in the Tiber, minus the three fingers of his right hand – once used to bless crowds and sign papal documents.

Some popes married, others had mistresses: in the early years of the 10th century, the illegitimate son of a union between Pope Sergius II and a Vatican matron was himself appointed pontiff.

Many of the Renaissance popes were decadent, but blessed with considerable financial know-how. The trade in indulgences – a 16th-century version of the present day derivatives market – proved particularly lucrative: the accumulated funds were used to build much of what is now the Vatican state, the world's smallest independent country.

Some popes became besotted with power, others went doolally.

Pius XII, pontiff from 1939 till 1958, showed increasing signs of instability in his declining years, locking himself away in his apartment and issuing directives on everything from how to conduct gynaecological examinations to developments in the Italian gas industry. He is said to have insisted on obedience at all times: Vatican staff were instructed to kneel when speaking to him on the phone.

To many, John Paul, when he became pope in 1978, was a breath of fresh air. He was the first non-Italian pontiff in 450 years. An inveterate traveller, he was part pop star and part stern disciplinarian who insisted on the infallibility of his authority, uncompromising on matters such as birth control and the bar on ordination of women priests.

"*Roma locuta, causa finita*" – Rome has spoken, the case is closed – was the refrain.

John Paul was a veteran of more than 80 trips overseas by the time he embarked on what was considered a groundbreaking visit to Cuba in 1998. At the age of 77, he had Parkinson's disease and was still suffering from the after-effects of being shot four times in a 1981 assassination attempt.

But Karol Wojtyla was still a global superstar. In Havana, the world's media was waiting.

A big story – for a day
Havana, 1998

The US TV anchorman – perfectly-combed hair, permatan glowing in the Caribbean sun – can hardly contain his excitement.

"It's gotta be one of the biggest events of the century. Just think of it – Communism meets Catholicism, Fidel and John Paul.

"Everyone's going mad for the story."

We're sitting on the steps of Revolution Square in central Havana, watching as final preparations are made for a mass the Pope will say in a few days' time.

At one end of the square is a giant representation of Jesus Christ. At the other there's an equally large portrait of Che Guevara. The US media is here in force. Thousands of dollars have been spent flying in TV film crews, along with their giant pantechnicons. Generators chug away; blond women with whiter-than-white teeth practise microphone soundbites.

Pope John Paul is making his first visit to Cuba. After the pontiff steps gingerly down the plane steps, he and Fidel Castro – dressed not in his usual combat outfit but in a double-breasted early 1950s-style demob suit – stretch out their arms and embrace.

The hero of the Cuban revolution – schooled by the Jesuits – is only a few years younger than the Pope but, in the body language, John Paul is the father, greeting a favourite, if rather difficult and wayward eldest son.

The crowd sings hymns to a salsa beat as the Pope rides into Havana. The evening sun, the colour of ripe corn, shines on the capital's once-handsome, now crumbling, Spanish mansions. A coach full of nodding bishops goes by. A group of mulatto girls in figure-hugging jeans and T-shirts clap and dance.

Schoolchildren chant "Juan Pablo secundo. Te quiere todo ei mundo" – John Paul the second. All the world loves you.

Next morning, there's a flurry of activity in the hotel lobby, with piles of TV kit being loaded onto trolleys. The tanned anchor man is dashing out the door.

"Gotta get back to Washington," he shouts, waving a clipboard. "All sorts of shit going on."

The US media circus is moving on. The story of the century has been shoved aside. Back home, Monica Lewinsky is spilling the beans about a sexual liaison in the White House with Bill Clinton. It's goodbye John Paul and Fidel, hello Monica and Bill.

A depressed-looking US bishop in charge of the Vatican's communications team diplomatically describes the American evacuation as "an unfortunate indicator of priorities". The rest of us are relieved: in the more relaxed, less media-frenzied atmosphere, with the Pope off touring the island, there's time for some R&R.

"If only they could see us back home now," says Father Tom, part of an Irish clerical delegation following in John Paul's footsteps.

Father Tom is a tall, imposing figure with a bald, shiny brown head, the shape of a farmyard egg. We stand in the corner of a small Havana bar, mojitos stuffed with greenery on the marble counter. The rain thunders down on the corrugated iron roof; overworked gutters spew pools of water into the narrow alley outside.

"Here we are, drinking mosquitoes, puffing on stogies, leading the life of Hemingway – it's not all bad, is it?" says Tom.

We wobble our way to the apartment of a friend of Tom's for dinner. She is a jolly, red-faced, left-leaning Italian – a teacher married to a local engineer. His main job is servicing the lifts in Havana's ageing hotels. In a mix of Spanish, Italian and English, the mechanical quirks and intricacies of various brands are discussed.

"The old Schindler lift, she is good," he says, hands describing cogs, sprockets and pulleys. "But the early Otis – she is the best."

Every day there's a new challenge. The long-running US embargo on exports to Cuba means parts have to be carefully refashioned and repaired.

"I am engineer, but also inventor," says the lift man. "I am very proud to see my lifts still going up and down."

The apartment is on one floor of a grand, now crumbling

mansion built by *criollos*, the old land-owning aristocracy. There's a marble staircase, tiles from Andalusia, wooden floors brought from Barcelona, and stained glass red and yellow fanlights. A warm wind blows in from the Gulf of Mexico. Bowls of pasta are passed round. Glasses of rum are refilled.

The engineer's mother, a sparkly 85-year-old, emerges from a back room. In the early days of the revolution, she was with Fidel in the Sierra Maestra mountains, translating incoming radio broadcasts, sending out messages in English. She talks of 1959 and riding in a jeep with El Comandante on his way into a newly-liberated Havana.

"He says to the people that he smells, that his hair and beard are dirty – but they kiss and hug him. He is the same as the Pope – or maybe even Jesu Christo."

We, minus mother-in-law, go off dancing. The Lada taxi looks as though it's just finished last in the Omsk stock car races. There's no exhaust and the windows are missing.

Halfway along the Malecón, the once-majestic but now dilapidated Havana waterfront, there's a malfunction somewhere in the Lada's innards.

Two young women in tight white trousers appear out of the darkness to give us a push. We're all laughing like schoolkids on an outing. Prostitution is officially banned in Cuba, but during the Pope's visit the girls are out in force.

"Havana is like a woman in love," says my guide book, published in 1941. "Eager to give pleasure, she will be anything you want her to be – exciting or peaceful, gay or quiet, brilliant or tranquil."

The *Palacio de Salsa* is packed. Every step a Cuban takes is a dance. Waiters boogie woogie to the table. Matrons waggle enormous backsides in sensuous rhythm.

Castro was once expounding on the way capitalist corporations seduce consumers. He ran his hand down a bottle of Coca-Cola. "You close your eyes and immediately you dream of the body of a woman."

Next day, bleary-eyed and joints aching from a salsa overdose, we're back on the papal trail, catching the last few hours of the pontiff's visit. John Paul, with Castro sitting close, wags an admonishing finger at the Cuban regime and calls for more religious freedom. But he also rails against what he calls "blind market forces" and the extremes of capitalism.

The Pope pauses at the top of the aircraft steps and turns to give a final wave.

El Comandante flutters his long fingers in farewell. His wispy beard blows sideways in the wind. The door on the papal plane closes with a swish.

Fidel raises his face to the rainy sky. For a moment, the old communist takes on the gaunt look of a saint in an El Greco painting.

"Once a Jesuit, always a Jesuit," says Father Tom.

*****

Monsignor T is a close friend and confidant, blessed with a mischievous sense of humour. Over a modest lunch, he talks of a visit he made some years previously to a discreet clerical outfitters tucked away in a London mews. The shop catered for all branches of Christianity.

"I was collecting a clerical suit – my first new one in at least two decades – when I spotted a rather unusual frock coat on a hanger: it was of considerable proportions and had two little pockets at the back.

"Enquiring of the fitter, I was told it was awaiting collection by the Reverend Ian Paisley." The Monsignor pauses to take a pinch of snuff from a small silver box. Concerned that he might be divulging something a little naughty, he has to be prompted to continue the tale.

"I really don't know what came over me, but I'd just returned from Rome and happened to have a papal medal in my wallet.

"I extracted it and placed it in one of the pockets of the Reverend Paisley's jacket."

The Monsignor brushes some snuff grains from his jacket.

"Rather a silly thing to do, don't you think?" A boyish smile lights up his face.

The tailoring tale came to mind some years later when, walking down a street in Rome, I came across an unusual line of shops.

The Pope's tailor
Rome, 2004

At first glance, the shops along the Via Santa Chiara, just off the Piazza Minerva in central Rome, look little different to many others in the Italian capital.

The displays are elegant. The lighting is subdued. The old, ornate storefronts are freshly painted. What sets these stores apart are the goods on offer.

There are crosses and rosary beads, chalices and small travelling cases – not for clothes but for miniature pop-up mass kits designed for the busy priest on the go. Varieties of incense are on sale: the odour is intoxicating.

One shop stands alone at the end of the street. Gammarelli is the *meglio di tutto*, or bee's knees, of the clerical outfitting business. It is the Pope's tailor.

Beneath a sign saying '*Sartoria Per Ecclesiastici*', the window display is sparse: a small selection of vestments, a pair of uncomfortable-looking black buckled shoes, a red stole, and a few elaborately-embroidered cotton handkerchiefs. But then cast an eye over to the corner and there's the unmistakable sign of Gammarelli's special position in the clerical clothing hierarchy: a solitary *zucchetto* – the small, white skullcap worn by the Pope.

A bell tinkles as the door is opened. Rows of small wooden drawers stretch to the ceiling. There's a long, broad counter onto which bolts of dark cloth are slapped with resounding thuds, ready for cutting.

Immaculately-suited men bustle about, tape measures round their necks. There's a whiff of expensive aftershave. Staff and merchandise are as one, all crisp and perfectly formed.

Pictures of famous customers stare down from the wall. They're not film stars or sports personalities, but somber-looking portraits of popes past and present.

Gammarelli not only dresses the Pope: it also serves other clerics – cardinals in their flaming red robes, monsignors in deep purple, and cindery black for country priests.

Call it eccentricity, call it a faintly ridiculous fashion statement, but for years I've favoured wearing red socks. The trouble is they're not always easy to come by, not in the right shade anyway.

Once, in the midst of a rather tedious European Union conference, a French foreign minister confided that the place to buy such things was at Gammarelli.

"Ask," he said, "for the same socks as a cardinal."

I take a deep, nervous breath and approach the counter.

Italy is considered to be the centre of the world's fashion industry, and the Catholic Church is not immune to changing tastes. At one time, not so long ago, bishops would dress in long robes, a train of shimmering silk drifting after them. In the old days, tassels, pom-poms and fancy hats were two a penny.

But then came Vatican II – the great ecclesiastical council of the 1960s – where it was decided the Church should move closer to the people and more into the modern age.

Many of the old rituals were done away with. The order came from on high that the pomp associated with fancy vestments and other finery had to go.

Is it possible, I ask the smiling man behind the counter, for those who are not clerics to make purchases here?

The Gammarelli family has been running their shop for six generations. Maximillian Gammarelli, the present-day manager, could not be more obliging.

"Certainly," he says. "And what exactly would sir be requiring?"

"Well, I was rather keen on buying a pair of red socks," I say.

Steps are fetched and Maximillian ascends to the heights.

Interestingly, there's a reappraisal going on concerning the changes ushered in by Vatican II. There are those who feel the Church, in losing some of its rituals, has also lost status – and it's mystery.

Some say the Mass itself, in certain parts of the world, has been allowed to become little more than a 'happy-clappy' piece of entertainment. There are calls for preserving Church traditions – and talk of the old vestments and hats being brought out of the closet.

A package is placed on the counter. The tissued covering is peeled back to reveal a flaming red pair of knee-length socks. Maximillian asks me to clench my fist while the foot of the sock is curled around. The method of measuring guarantees a perfect fit, he says.

The label on the socks is in English: "Gentleman socks," it says. "Wash in tepid water with neutral soap."

Maximillian takes time to expertly wrap my purchase. I'm concerned about stopping the normal flow of clerical business. The Pope is unlikely to stroll in looking for a new robe, but maybe a bishop is waiting to be served.

"Anytime you require replacements, you are most welcome to visit Gammarelli," says Maximillian.

The socks cost a little over nine euros. I take two pairs and walk, a little ecclesiastically, out into the Rome sunshine.

Postscript

Cotton College has been closed for several years. Not so long ago, I returned for the first time in more than a half century. The dormitory windows were broken, the classrooms filled with green pools of stagnant water. The church we spent so much time in had a picture of snarling Alsatian dogs on its door and a "Dangerous, do not enter" sign.

My early involuntary flirtation with the priesthood did come in handy many years later.

A friend in California was getting married. He rang up, offering the airfare to attend the wedding. There was only one catch: I had to do the marrying.

Everything is possible in America, especially in California: courtesy of the internet and a payment of US$50, I was 'ordained' into a church in the state, taking the rank of Monsignor.

The ceremony was performed at a winery. A little nervous, I had to be prompted to ask the bride if she agreed to have and hold. My church is in frequent contact, with news of the latest fashions in clerical clothing and reminders that, as a minister, I am empowered to carry out not only weddings but also baptisms and funerals, even ordinations.

Despite increasing frailty, John Paul continued to travel in the years up to his death in 2005, aged 84, making more than 100 foreign tours – more trips abroad than all previous popes combined.

Karol Wojtyla's legacy is mixed: on one hand, he brought new life into the Church, popularising it around the world. On the other hand, he was unbending on most matters of dogma and made sure to stack the Curia – the Vatican bureaucracy – with conservatives and appoint cardinals and bishops who would continue to abide by his strict doctrinal views.

Fidel Castro died in 2016, to be succeeded by his brother.

Gammarelli is still very much in business. My cardinal's socks have had several outings – although, as a result of frequent washes, they've gone slack. Maybe it's time for another trip to Rome to purchase some clerical garters to keep them up.

CHAPTER 9

Ireland

Shoot-out at the cemetery • Tea with the Taoiseach
The airport hearse • Charlie dreams in Morse
Wittgenstein's puzzled chickens

There is something surreal – almost comic – about being shot at in a cemetery.

I'd arrived in Dublin in late 1987 as correspondent for the *Financial Times*. Up till that time, Ireland for me had been a playground, full of childhood holidays on deserted beaches in Kerry, swims in icy Atlantic waters, and rambles across stone-walled fields in Roscommon.

With my mother, there'd been a seemingly endless stream of relatives serving up lashings of tea and mountains of ham sandwiches in parlours with sad Sacred Hearts mounted on yellow walls.

With my father, it was glasses of red lemonade in the corner of dark, sawdust-floored bars, watching as pints were swilled by men in battered brown trilbies smelling of hay and fried breakfasts.

Now I was cowering behind a gravestone in a Belfast cemetery, bullets ricocheting off the stonework. This was a serious business.

The Milltown murders
Belfast, 1988

A grey mist shrouds the city. A bitter wind blows pockets of rain in from the Irish Sea. A tin can bounces down the road, echoing off the walls of the back-to-back houses.

A group of us reporters are among thousands thronging the streets in Republican West Belfast, shuffling along like soldiers in a defeated army towards Milltown cemetery, the area's main burial ground.

Three IRA members – two men and a woman – had been gunned down by the SAS in Gibraltar while plotting, said the British, a bomb attack on a military band.

The bodies of the three had been flown back to Dublin and then transported at night to the North. The media had followed the extended funeral journey; at one stage, the hearses had been stoned by Protestant loyalists.

The faces around the Republican plot in Milltown are pale and pinched, as if they've never seen the sun. There's a lot of black leather about. The police and military aren't on the ground, but overhead their helicopters are watching and filming, whirring and clacking like an angry parliament of rooks.

The coffins – each draped in the Irish tricolor, with the IRA's symbolic bouquet of black gloves and beret on top – are lined up on trolleys by the freshly-cut graves.

The families gather round, squashed between tombstones. A young boy, pale and parched, looks on, shivering. There are muttered prayers and responses, the sound rising and falling like the buzz of bees round a hive.

The flag from one of the coffins is removed with military precision, ceremoniously folded and presented to a relative. The well-shined wooden box is lowered on straps into the grave. As it thuds to the bottom, there are a series of muffled explosions.

Panic. Some stand, perplexed. Most hit the ground as if struck by a giant wave, spread-eagling themselves across graves or huddling behind stone crosses.

Grenades are going off. There's the sound of gunshots.

Gerry Adams, glasses askew, grabs a megaphone. He stands up. "Keep down, keep calm," he shouts.

Martin McGuinness – a senior figure in the British military once told me that he regarded the head of the Derry IRA as "good officer material" – is leaping over a tombstone, directing operations.

In the midst of all the confusion, instinct rather than analysis takes over. I have the idea that the Republican bigwigs are the main target of the attack and that it would be best to get as far away from them as possible.

Others have the same idea; we dodge between tombstones, leap over graves. The trouble is we're running towards the gunfire, not away from it.

Michael Stone, the Milltown bomber, is an unlikely-looking urban guerrilla. As he runs away down the edge of the graveyard, he cuts a comic figure, his waddling backside and short legs not really up to the task, more Oliver Hardy than Rambo.

Every so often, Stone pauses to turn and fire at his pursuers. His long, tangled hair streams after him as he makes for a motorway at the bottom of the graveyard. At one point, his flat tweed cap falls off. The crowd is catching up: this time he doesn't stop but climbs up onto the roadway.

Stone is just about to be swallowed up by his pursuers when a police Land Rover appears. He is bundled inside and whisked away.

Three people are dead and more than 60 injured as a result of the bombings and shooting.

A young woman, dark make-up smudged across her ashen face, lies against a tombstone, staring up at the sky. An elderly man, a monk's white rim of hair circling his bald head, has his arms wrapped round two young boys, their bodies convulsed with shakes.

Corpses and the injured are loaded into hearses that, only a short time before, had brought the coffins of the IRA trio into the cemetery.

The whole event – which quickly became known as the 'Milltown Massacre' – is filmed and shown around the world. In the following days, bloody event follows bloody event in what is one of the worst weeks of 'The Troubles'.

A funeral is held for one of those killed at Milltown. For reasons still unknown, two British off-duty soldiers drive into the funeral cortege. Apparently realising the danger they were in at the last minute, they try to reverse and escape. Shots are fired, but the crowd gathers round. The soldiers are dragged out of their car and killed.

In the midst of all the mayhem, I have an interview with Sir Jack Hermon, head of what was then called the Royal Ulster Constabulary. Getting into the inner sanctum at police HQ is a lengthy process. Names tell a lot in Northern Ireland: there are not many Kierans about in the Protestant-dominated RUC. I'm searched, then searched again.

Sir Jack is a big man with a shiny red face and a crushing handshake. It seems he's favoured me with an interview due to the mistaken impression that, as a *Financial Times* reporter, I might be able to give advice on his stocks and shares.

We quickly move on to other subjects. Sir Jack is concerned about Northern Ireland's image.

"Mr Cooke," he says, "there are a few things you should know about life here north of the border."

Sir Jack's teeth whistle as he talks. He grips my thigh with one of his giant hands.

"We Ulster people are very law-abiding people. We are very honest people. We are very hospitable people."

There's a lengthy pause. There is something messianic about Sir Jack's stare. "It's just that we have the unfortunate habit of killing each other."

Tea with Charlie
Dublin, 1990

In the late 1980s, Charlie Haughey was running the show south of the border. It was a bleak period, an era of big cutbacks in government spending and rising unemployment. Once again, thousands were emigrating in search of jobs.

As Taoiseach, or prime minister, Haughey had – to put it mildly – a chequered reputation.

To some, he was a hero – a leader who stood up to Margaret Thatcher, increased Ireland's standing in Europe, and laid the foundations for the country's economic growth.

To many others, he personified all that was rotten in Irish political life – a master manipulator and an all-round financial scoundrel, an oligarch rather than a statesman, prepared to do any number of dirty deals in order to feather his own nest and remain in power.

Haughey did not like the media. He was particularly averse to the British press.

*****

Long before arriving to work in Dublin, I'd heard the stories. They were not all bad. One in particular – probably apocryphal – cast Haughey in a favourable light.

The setting was Inishvickillane, the island Haughey owned off the coast of County Kerry.

A team of builders went out to the island to do some repairs to the Haughey holiday residence.

An Atlantic storm swept in. The builders were trapped on the island for three days, in the course of which they happened on a cellar. Haughey enjoyed the good life: the cellar was stuffed full of the finest wines.

The lads were understandably thirsty. The Château Lafite went down well, as did the Petrus. Later, the Château d'Yquem served as a decent nightcap.

The foreman eventually made it out to the island and was horrified to find not only a severely hungover group of labourers, but also a noticeably depleted stock of wine. After some thought, he decided the best thing to do was to go into the supermarket on the mainland and buy replacement bottles.

As a consequence, a line of Blue Nun – the Liebfraumilch sweet German wine mass produced in the 1970s and 80s – came to rest alongside the esteemed wines of Bordeaux, Burgundy and Alsace in the Taoiseach's cellar.

The story is that Haughey, when he learned of what happened, laughed the incident off. Whether he ever drank the Blue Nun is not known.

PJ Mara, the government spokesman, was Haughey's gatekeeper. Every Tuesday morning, we – a small band of Dublin-based foreign correspondents – would go to PJ's office and drink watery coffee out of elegant government crockery.

He was a born entertainer and storyteller. His briefings were amusing – and hopeless as a source of news.

A BBC intern fresh from London came along on one occasion. PJ was his usual, ebullient self, describing the surprising hobbies of the wife of a certain ambassador, the ignorance of one minister, the terrible taste of another.

The intern was becoming restless, keen to have a story. The government in London had just appointed Sir Patrick Mayhew, an old-school Tory Party grandee, as Secretary of State for Northern Ireland.

What, asked the intern, was the Irish government's view of Sir Patrick's appointment?

PJ leant back in his chair, rubbed his eyes and breathed deeply. "Sir Patrick is it? That feckin' gobshite."

The intern's pen froze in mid-air. She left the briefing without a story: using the word gobshite on the one o'clock news just wouldn't do.

After many months of quiet persuasion, and more than a few drinking sessions, PJ arranged an interview for me with Haughey. The encounter was not a success. A good interview needs some revelation or show of emotion, a spark to bring the encounter to life. There was none of that with Haughey.

A detailed list of questions had to be submitted beforehand and I was warned about any deviations from the script.

In the early 1970s, Haughey was thrown out of government, accused of being involved in a plot to smuggle arms to the IRA in Northern Ireland. As I prepare to meet the great man, PJ whispers that if I so much as hint at those IRA-related events he'll have my guts for garters.

The first five minutes of the encounter are used up as the Taoiseach makes an elaborate show of serving tea out of a tall silver pot, fussing round with the air of a man who has never had to carry out such duties.

Meanwhile, all the talk is of Europe. Ireland is about to assume the presidency of the EU.

Haughey is a keen sailor: he has the air of a skipper about him, hand on the tiller, guiding the European ship through troubled international waters.

"There is a particular understanding between myself and President Mitterand," says the Taoiseach, struggling to manipulate the sugar tongs. "We have become close friends over the years."

Haughey also has a soft spot for President Gorbachev. It's as if he's head boy, putting ticks against the names of prefects he trusts to do his bidding.

I attempt to steer the conversation to domestic matters, to the struggling economy, to the many thousands still being forced to leave the country. There is silence. The script has been abused. Haughey's eyelids come down like shop shutters.

I blunder on. What does he think of the continuing violence in Northern Ireland? Is there any chance of peace talks being revived?

The questions are ignored. I might as well have been asking about a dust-up in the Caucasus or a change of government in Botswana.

Irish men are not renowned as stylish dressers. Haughey is different. His suit is expertly tailored, the shirt of the finest cotton.

More tea is poured. The milk smells slightly off.

Haughey shows me a picture of Mitterand and himself standing on a windswept beach. I presume it's on Inishvickillane. The French president, never one to waste a smile, has the look of a man wishing he was somewhere else.

The rain peppers the panes on the tall Georgian office window. Dublin is granite grey. Haughey is elsewhere.

"I regard the south of France as the epitome of the development of modern civilization – I think the French have whatever is necessary for a good life."

It's said like a pronouncement from on high – a great quote for a holiday brochure, but hardly the stuff of front page headlines.

I try once again to focus on affairs closer to home. What about IRA smuggling operations across the Irish border? Does the Irish government have any concerns about allegations of a British 'shoot to kill' policy in Northern Ireland?

Once again, the eyelids come down. The Taoiseach grabs the arms of his chair. The interview is at an end. There's a momentary spark of life as, being shown to the door, French wines are mentioned.

Haughey assumes a far-off look. "I have always had a great appreciation for them," he says. His handshake is limp and cold.

My notebook is filled with aimless squiggles. I'm tempted to ask the Taoiseach about Inishvikillane and the Blue Nun, but the moment passes.

Last stop Knock
County Mayo, 2006

Knock airport, in County Mayo in the west of Ireland, is one of the world's more obscure international termini. Opened in the mid-1980s, the airport is miles from the nearest city, surrounded by small walled fields and cattle pens.

A local priest, Monsignor James Horan, had single-handedly bamboozled politicians and bankers into financing the project; the aim was both to facilitate pilgrimages to a nearby shrine and also to connect the relatively isolated surrounding area with the outside world.

The Monsignor was a good wheeler-dealer; despite the naysayers' doubts, the airport, built on a soggy, foggy stretch of bog, has been a success, with nearly a million passengers flying in and out each year in pre-Covid times.

Many leave from Knock in search of work and a new life overseas. Incoming flights often carry former emigrants back, making a final journey home.

✶✶✶✶✶

Emerging from the small arrivals hall at Knock, there's the rather unnerving sight of a funeral hearse and a crowd of black-clad mourners. The wind whips around. A soft rain falls. Men with ruddy red faces – farmers' arms squeezed into suit jackets – stand about. Sombrely-dressed women chat quietly.

A discreet enquiry reveals a sad but frequently heard tale: "It's Michael Joe," says the hearse driver, face like polished marble. "Left here in the late 1950s when he was 25; always meant to come back to settle but never made it – not till now."

For years, Michael Joe worked on building sites in London, and later – along with many thousands of other Irish men – constructed Britain's schools, hospitals and motorways.

There were songs about these tough labourers. The spoken preamble to Dominic Behan's song *McAlpine's Fusliers* includes the lines:

"You'll stand behind the mixer
Until your skin is turned to tan
And they'll say, Good on you, Paddy,
With your boat fare in your hand."

But Michael Joe and many others didn't catch that boat. Every month, he'd send money home to the small family farm. A lifelong bachelor, Michael Joe didn't take proper care of himself. In old age, he ended up living alone in a London bedsit. Now, as part of his final request, he's being flown back for burial in the village he left all those years ago.

Emigration has been an integral part of Irish life for generations. In the US alone, more than 33 million people – about 10 per cent of the population – claim Irish ancestry.

Rita, my mother, left the small family farm in the west of Ireland in 1936 to cross to England and train as a nurse. She was just shy of her 18th birthday: she had not even been to Dublin before that trip.

A decade before, her father had gone to the US, building skyscrapers in Chicago. When the Great Depression hit, he came home, little money saved and a virtual stranger to his family. One of the six children had died while he was away.

Jerry Cowley, a medical doctor recently turned politician in the west of Ireland, says Ireland owes a tremendous debt to Michael Joe and the tens of thousands of others forced to leave in search of work.

"There are so many similar cases – both men and women – who went off abroad, sending money back home and keeping this country afloat during its dark days."

Some years ago, Dr Cowley and a few others decided to do something about the plight of this largely forgotten generation of Irish emigrants. Through voluntary contributions at first, and later by persuading the Irish government to put in some funding, a scheme was started to bring these people home, giving them accommodation and a welcome back into the community.

Under what's called the 'Safe Home' scheme, nearly 400 elderly Irish people – from Britain, the US, Australia and South Africa – have so far been settled back in Ireland.

"Of course, many Irish have built lives overseas and are happily settled abroad, but there's this large group that always hankered after coming home," says Dr Cowley.

"They contributed to Ireland's national coffers for years. And their labours, in large part ignored, laid the foundations for Ireland's present day success. The least we can do is give them a home in the twilight of their lives."

Mary Caffrey is a sparky 75-year-old. She left the family home in County Mayo in the early 1950s. There followed years of working as a maid in houses round Britain, sending meagre savings back home. Eventually, she found herself living alone in Glasgow. Though the family she saved so much for had died out, Mary still yearned to return to Ireland. She applied to the 'Safe Home' scheme, and now lives in an immaculately-kept apartment in the small village of Mulranny in County Mayo, on the edge of the Atlantic.

"When I called with the news that there was a place here for her she said she'd come right away," says Dr Cowley. "She'd had her bags packed for two years – that's how anxious she was to come back."

Father George Ennis is an 80-year-old Catholic priest who was based in London for years, mostly as a chaplain to a number of psychiatric hospitals.

"It was very tough work and in the end took a toll on my health," he says. "The only thing that kept me going was a two-week fishing holiday back in Ireland each year."

Father George is also a resident at the settlement in Mulranny. "I thought I had died and gone to heaven when I came here," says the priest, face creased with a smile. "And I can fish, every day, all I want."

Of course, Ireland has changed a great deal over the years. For some, dreams of the old, idealised, carefree life at home don't always match present-day realities.

Mary Caffrey and Father George are the fortunate ones.

Back at Knock airport, Michael Joe's body is transferred into the waiting hearse. The soft rain has turned into a downpour. Drenched mourners stand to respectful attention. A wreath of white lilies flies loose, cartwheeling in the whipping wind across the car park.

A funeral attendant gives chase, like a rugby player running after an awkwardly-bouncing ball.

Coffin inside, the hearse door is shut with a thud. It's a homecoming of sorts, but not the one Michael Joe would have wanted.

Charlie pulls the pints
Louisburgh, 2006

The bar has long been a centerpiece of social life in Ireland.

Louisburgh, our local town perched on County Mayo's Atlantic seaboard, has a population of about 430, but until recently six bars competed for customers on the town's two streets. Back in the 1960s, there were more than twice that number.

A combination of emigration, drink-driving regulations, declining economic fortunes and, in recent times, the curse of Covid has radically altered drinking habits.

Gaffneys was one of Louisburgh's more popular drinking places. Charlie Gaffney, its owner, was a figure of considerable stature.

*****

When Charlie eventually gave up tending behind the bar, Gaffneys pub gave a final beer and whiskey-soaked sigh, shut its doors, closed its cellar one last time – and died.

Gaffneys, just off Louisburgh's main street, was not in any way special – it was much like one of the many drinking establishments that once lined towns and villages all over Ireland.

In days gone by, every other shop would be a pub. In addition, just in case a raging thirst would suddenly seize the unwary shopper, the grocer would have a beer pump on the counter alongside the bacon slicer – and bottles of spirits lined up on the shelves between the tins of baked beans and peas.

Yet Gaffneys was special. It was the bar where we – garrulous journalists, dubious property developers, risqué finance experts, down-at-heel writers, farmers and fisher people – would gravitate to, a fixture in the town as much as the church on the bend or the newsagents down the street.

There would be a sod of turf on the fire – gently smoking away, but scarcely throwing out any heat. The bar stools were scuffed, the wooden chair seats like mirrors, polished by a thousand backsides.

Long before community centres were established, bars like Gaffneys would function as places to carry out important local business.

Charlie – his mother bought the bar in the early years of the last century, and his father was the local policeman – was a power in the town, tasked with keeping an unofficial eye on things, helping sort out disputes, issuing fishing licences.

In one corner, there was a statue of the Virgin Mary; stern old family portraits hung on the wall. By way of contrast, there were also pictures of long-legged models draped about Gaffneys in a series of sensuous poses – an imaginative fashion photographer had once arranged a photo shoot in the bar.

At certain times of the year, Gaffneys would be full – conversation and laughter echoing off its green and cream-coloured walls. At other times, particularly in the depths of winter when the dampness of the surrounding boglands and the sea mists would envelop the town, only Charlie would be present.

He was not a 'hail fellow, well met' type of landlord – far from it.

As you curled round the door, Charlie would be sitting in his usual position behind the bar, chin cupped in hand, cigarette between nicotine-stained fingers, eyes watering in the smoke.

He'd be puzzling over 23 across or 10 down – Charlie was a crossword addict.

A pint would start to be poured, then allowed to settle. Minutes would go by – you might exchange a few comments on the weather or discuss the prospects for fishing, but, like matches held to damp paper, the spark of conversation would soon die away.

Drink delivered and duty done, Charlie would return to the important business of solving the anagram of 15 down, the only sound the ticking of the bar room clock.

Silence is a precious, often undervalued commodity – and Charlie had plenty of it.

When he was younger, with no jobs on offer locally, he'd gone off to sea, joining the British merchant navy. Perhaps it was there, working as a radio officer, he learned to embrace silence.

Travelling the world, deep in the bowels of the ship – with only the churning of engines and creaking of the hull for company – Charlie would sit, alone for hours on end, doing the crossword, smoking, waiting for the radio to give its messages, most in the old dot-dot-dashes of Morse code.

Charlie once admitted to having dreams in Morse. When, a few years ago, the code was phased out, Charlie was upset – for him, it was like losing a language.

Perhaps he became more silent as the town around him changed; first, the local garage closed; then bars shut down and the old shops expanded into supermarkets.

Charlie died recently, aged 81. Years ago, he had returned to his native town, married and had given up his seafaring ways, inheriting the family pub.

Charlie's children, grown up now and with their own lives in Ireland and elsewhere, are reluctant to take on a job long out of fashion and with few prospects.

Michael Longley, the poet, was for many years a Gaffneys customer.

In a poem written in tribute to Charlie, he imagines what he calls "an ideal death", sitting at the bar, in company with its owner.

"I have just helped him to solve his crossword puzzle.
And we commune with ancestral photos in the alcove.
He doesn't notice that I am dead until closing time.
And he sweeps around my feet."

But it was Charlie who left the bar first.

Wittgenstein out West
Connemara, 2017

Generations of poets, writers and artists have travelled and lived in the west of Ireland, attracted by the ruggedness of the landscape, the clarity of its light, the tempestuousness of the storms – and its loneliness.

Heinrich Böll, the German writer who visited and lived on Achill Island off the coast of County Mayo in the 1950s, said the West was a place where you could play truant from Europe.

Ludwig Wittgenstein – considered by many to be among the greatest philosophers of the 20th century – also escaped westwards.

In the late 1940s, shortly before his death, Wittgenstein rented a cottage at a small harbour on the Killary, a 10-mile fjord that cuts like a shard of glass into Ireland's Atlantic coast in Connemara.

Once a week, Wittgenstein would cycle the long, windswept road over the bog to the post office in the village of Leenane to collect his books sent down from Dublin – heavy philosophical tomes and a selection of the latest whodunits. Otherwise, he tucked himself well away from the world.

*****

The philosopher's hideaway is not easy to find. The road winds and almost doubles back on itself. A turn-off to the right, past a grand house on a rhododendron-shrouded island where Oscar Wilde once stayed. Another right down a narrow, twisting lane and, finally, to a small harbour.

The windscreen wipers can hardly cope with the wind and driving rain, but then, as if a heavenly hand had flicked a switch, a lone spotlight of sun lights up the heather and bracken on the hillside.

Ludwig Wittgenstein, mathematician, engineer, architect and philosopher, hankered after solitude. He certainly found it here: a plaque on the side of a rather shabby-looking bungalow says that in 1948 he stayed six months in what is known as the Little Killary, writing up what would be his final work.

Born in Vienna into one of the richest families in Europe, Wittgenstein – brilliant, volatile and famously eccentric – turned his back on the moneyed life to study philosophy, eventually becoming a professor at Cambridge.

I'm trying to track down a local man, a fisherman who, it's said, might be able to tell me something about Wittgenstein's time out here on the fringes of Europe.

Doors are knocked on. A dog barks. Gulls shriek. A woman emerges from a caravan. "Mrs …?" I ask. "I could be," she answers, a mischievous smile on her face. In the west of Ireland, it's best not to ask too many direct questions. Nothing is hurried.

Her husband, the fisherman, appears: we discuss the weather, health problems, declining fish stocks, people we know. Connections are made. Finally, the subject of Wittgenstein is broached.

"My father, who used give him milk and spuds when he was here, said he was mad. You'd hardly get a word out of him.

"I wasn't born to see him, but my father would talk about the strange German who'd sit for hours on a rock, looking at the gulls," the fisherman recalls.

"It seems he was interested in how the birds flew because he was after designing a jet aircraft engine. He'd be taking notes and making drawings all the time."

Tea and chocolate biscuits are placed on the table. It's said Wittgenstein would work on his philosophy and other academic subjects all night – and spend the days ranging round the small fields criss-crossed with stone walls. He hardly ever slept.

"For all his strangeness, my father said he had a great way with nature – all the small birds would come and eat from his hand.

"After he left, I was put to sleep in the same bed Wittgenstein had. For 22 years that was my place." The fisherman's laugh turns into a deep-throated cough. "Not that any of his wild thinking rubbed off on me."

Wittgenstein, though he was a compulsive writer, produced relatively little published material. Few of his original manuscripts survive. His writings are precious, worth a small fortune these days.

There was talk that Wittgenstein left behind piles of notebooks in Ireland. Did your father come across any of them, I ask? Another cup of tea is poured. There are more chocolate biscuits.

"Come here till I tell you," says the fisherman leaning in close, a conspiratorial air about him.

"I remember a few years back, when my father was still alive, a taxi arrives up all the way from Dublin airport. A German book dealer says he'll pay thousands for just a scrap of your man's writing. Kept the taxi out there waiting for three hours.

"Now my father had to tell him: yes, there were notebooks and stacks of paper left by Wittgenstein. But what to do with them? Well, we kept poultry at the time, so…my father decides to use the whole lot as chicken litter."

The fisherman leans back, a faraway look in his eyes. "Not only was the book dealer mortified, so was my father. Imagine that – all that money gone so the chickens could be bedded down nice and comfortable."

Outside, the gulls wheel and squawk in the small harbour. Up on the hillside, sheep huddle by a stone wall, out of the wind.

Perhaps the great philosopher would have been pleased at how things worked out: Wittgenstein had little regard for his own work, saying what he wrote was not important – what was significant was what he didn't write.

Still, I wonder whether those hens appreciated what they were sleeping on. Perhaps they were enlightened? Or more likely, like me, just puzzled by the workings of a great mind.

Postscript

Michael Stone, the Milltown bomber, was sentenced to life imprisonment for the Belfast cemetery killings, but was released in 2000 under the terms of the Belfast Peace Agreement.

He then became something of a celebrity, selling his paintings and writing an autobiography. The jacket he wore at Milltown was auctioned at a loyalist club in Scotland for £10,000. He talked of peace; alongside Bishop Desmond Tutu, of South Africa, he took part in reconciliation discussions.

But it was not long before Stone, convicted of six murders at Milltown and elsewhere, reverted to his old ways. Armed with an imitation pistol and what was later described as a bag full of viable bombs, he entered the Northern Ireland parliament at Stormont, near Belfast. Security guards intercepted him by trapping his head in a revolving door.

At his trial, Stone insisted his antics were a piece of performance art, an explanation the judge dismissed as totally unconvincing. Stone was released on parole from prison in Northern Ireland in early 2021. A father of nine children from various liaisons, there are reports he recently married again.

Sir Jack Hermon died, aged 79, in 2008.

Charlie Haughey resigned as Taoiseach in 1992 amid accusations of interfering with the courts and bugging journalists' phones. Leaving office, he quoted from the closing lines of *Othello*: "I have done the state some service and they know't. No more of that."

It transpired that Haughey had done himself the most service of all, accepting million-pound gifts from businessmen that were paid into a slush fund in the Cayman Islands. Property, racehorses and paintings were bought and a regal lifestyle maintained.

Despite the revelations of financial shenanigans on a grand scale, Haughey never stood a full trial. When he died in 2006, at the age of 80, he was given a state funeral.

The hearses still line up outside the arrivals hall at Knock airport, with funeral directors offering a special 'repatriation service' to the families of those who have died in the UK or elsewhere abroad and who want to make their last journey home.

Unfortunately, Monsignor Horan did not live to see Knock realise its full potential. The first flight out of Knock was a pilgrimage to Lourdes, proudly led by the Monsignor. While in France, the cleric had a heart attack and died. The first scheduled flight into Knock brought the Monsignor's body back for burial.

The 'Safe Home' scheme has gone from strength to strength, helping settle many thousands of elderly, long-time emigrants back in Ireland.

"Dear Safe Home, I'm contacting you with my change of address," said a letter from a man who spent years working in the UK, now desperately wanting to return home to Galway. "I wish it (the address) was in Ireland. Please don't forget about me."

Gaffneys in Louisburgh is still there, though it's no longer a bar. Repainted a vivid pink, one of Charlie's daughters runs it as a restaurant in the summer months. The pictures of the ancestors – and the sensuous models – still hang on the walls.

Ludwig Wittgenstein died in early 1951, two years after his time spent in the West.

Little Killary hasn't changed much since the philosopher spent time there. There's a hostel for hikers, but otherwise little activity. A few hens amble about, the descendants of the pampered poultry that slept on the great man's notebooks. You can spot the pedigree; they have a slightly bewildered look about them.

CHAPTER 10:
Fine dining, strange smells

A fish head for Miss Marple · Lunch with Goldilocks
Dinner at the palace · Blancmange in a lavatory
The sniffer dog goes wild

Mosquitoes are making a pin cushion of the ankles. A woman shaped like a sumo wrestler on steroids stirs the contents of a giant wok.

Dishes clatter, jaws chomp. The pungent smell of spices is mixed with the fumes from passing buses, trucks and tuk tuks. After the years reporting in Greece and Ireland, we'd ricocheted back to the East, based this time in Malaysia.

Food, in all its infinite variety, is one of the great joys of living in Southeast Asia.

In a small park just off Kuala Lumpur's city centre, giant cauldrons of dark liquid bubble away, a fish head occasionally bobbing to the surface.

The practised nose of an old Asia hand wobbles in anticipation.

145

Feel the fire
Kuala Lumpur, 1995

The Margaret Rutherford lookalike leans in a little closer.

It's Miss Marple, confidentially imparting a vital clue she's uncovered. Her face – piercing blue eyes with folds below like theatre curtains – has the look of an excited bloodhound.

"There is nothing, absolutely nothing, like it." She pauses for dramatic effect. "A damn good curry. The hotter the better. We always had one for lunch in Indyah."

The nostrils and taste buds work overtime in Southeast Asia: chilli crabs by the sea in Singapore, satay at the roadside in Jakarta, steamed fish alongside a canal in Bangkok, spring rolls and mango salad on a Hanoi backstreet – these are the things that make life worthwhile, whatever the circumstances.

Miss Marple, the relation of a distant relation, manoeuvres herself – flowing, slightly-faded summer dress, shiny brogue shoes and stout chestnut walking stick – out of the taxi. Like a shark after its prey, she approaches the steaming tureens.

"Reggie, my late husband, insisted that a good curry was the king of any cuisine. He swore by them – said they'd kill any bugs in the system. He was particularly fond of a curry at lunchtime. Wash it down with a few cold beers, then retire for a little zizz and you'd be absolutely tip-top."

The tables are outside. The restaurant garden doubles as a meeting place for local bird fanciers. Aficionados stroll in with their feathered friends twittering away in elaborate bamboo cages. Birds are examined and discussed over lunch. It is the eastern equivalent of vintage car enthusiasts gathering in the car park of a country pub.

Miss Marple inhales deeply. Her eyes are streaming, her jowls flushed the colour of an autumn sunset.

"Ah, this is what I've been waiting for. I do so wish Reggie was here."

Successive waves of immigrants to the region have brought their cuisines to Southeast Asia. In turn, these dishes have been blended with local dishes.

At the turn of the 20th century, large numbers of Indians – mainly Tamils from southern India – were brought in to what was then Malaya by the British colonialists to work the rubber and tea plantations. They brought their fish-head curry with them.

The dish is not to everyone's taste, but veterans of the curry circuit – distinguishable by their fiery breath and slightly mad eyes – swear by it. Crack your teeth on one of those craniums and you are hooked, they declare.

Miss Marple doesn't hesitate. She selects one of the biggest fish heads available.

"The eyes are white and popping out," she says. "That means it's nice and fresh."

The Indian cook nods approvingly. He knows a fish head expert when he sees one.

A large banana leaf, pressed and pristine, is laid on the table. A generous pile of white rice, which serves as an antidote to the fire of the curry, is ladled onto the leaf. The fish head and accompanying sauce are then placed on top.

Westerners might chose to jettison the fish head early on, preferring to eat just the sauce and rice. Locals know better: the tastiest, smoothest flesh is found round the eyes, cheeks and gills.

Miss Marple is digging away like a deranged brain surgeon.

"So many people are squeamish when it comes to food," she says, attention concentrated on an eyeball that would not look out of place on a billiard table.

"I don't believe in wasting anything. Do be a gent and order another beer."

The delicate diner will often choose to use a fork and spoon, but the correct way to tackle a curry is with the hand, usually the right.

The rice is squeezed into balls, then dipped in the curry sauce.

Flesh and pieces of vegetable are lowered into the mouth, like a bird feeding its young.

There's a basin in the corner for a much-needed post-curry wash and brush up.

We rise, a little unsteadily. Miss Marple showers compliments on the cook. He looks like an embarrassed schoolboy awarded first place in the class poetry competition.

"Reggie always said he could judge how good a curry was by how quickly he went to sleep," says the relation of a relation. "Sometimes he'd just doze off right there at the table."

Tummies doing the hokey cokey, we bounce off in the taxi. The sound of satisfied, snuffling snoring soon punctuates the air.

Chicken at the Vatican
Kuala Lumpur, 1994

Like the Tamil migrants from southern India, the various groups of Chinese who moved south to escape famine and poverty at home and settle in Southeast Asia brought their own distinctive cuisines with them.

Nowadays, some of that culinary variety is being lost.

College-educated sons and daughters of ageing proprietors don't want to spend time slaving over red-hot woks or giant saucepans of noodles. Many of the old-style eating places have closed.

What were called corner coffee shops were once present on every street, stalls serving a variety of dishes. They were establishments that overwhelmed the palate – and severely tested the eardrums.

*****

Locals call it the Vatican, but no one seems to know why.

The coffee shop sits on a busy corner in the old section of Kuala Lumpur, its wooden swing doors clack-clacking back and forth.

The barman, head covered in a bristle of grey hair, is called Goldilocks.

A portly Indian gent in grey flannels, silk flowing from the top pocket of his blue blazer, comes in and parks his ample backside on a polished bar stool.

"Hey, Goldilocks," he shouts above the coffee shop din. "Give me a Johnny Walker Black Label, on the rocks. Roger, over and out."

Goldilocks, dressed in the usual Chinese catering kit of a pair of freshly-laundered baggy blue shorts and white singlet, springs into action.

His clogs do a slap-slap dance across the greasy floor. He simultaneously pours the whisky, pulls the top off a bottle of beer and strains a jug of coffee through what looks like a bull's scrotum.

A battered tin on a pulley and string is pulled down from the ceiling. Notes are stuffed in, change given. There are no bills, no receipts.

An elderly European, a retired plantation manager, sits at a round, marble-topped table, nursing a beer. He has thin arms and yellowing skin. The cigarette in his hand shakes.

The Vatican bar is like a club. The Indian whisky drinker is addressing no one in particular.

"That damn Sikh, he's an absolute blackguard and rogue – thoroughly untrustworthy, never bowls a straight ball…"

The rest of the coffee shop is getting on with its business. To one side of the entrance is a battered desk displaying jars of pickled ginger and sweets. Behind it sits the *towkay*, or boss man, of the establishment.

The *towkay* is elderly; he has a single foot-long white hair hanging from his chin. While cleaning his ears with what looks like a miniature chimney brush, he keeps a careful eye on everything that's going on, counting every dish and every coin.

He, like Goldilocks, is dressed in baggy shorts and singlet. But don't be fooled. He's probably a millionaire, a swanky brace of cars parked in the garage, children at Harvard and Oxbridge.

Most of the old-style coffee shops in Malaysia and Singapore have traditionally been run by the descendants of immigrants who came from the island of Hainan, off the south coast of China.

The Hainanese migrated south later than most of their fellow Chinese: by the time they arrived on the Malay peninsula in the late 19th century, many of the more lucrative jobs in tin mining or in the textile trade were no longer available. The Hainanese concentrated on catering, particularly for the British military.

No colonial house was without its Hainanese 'houseboy' – white jackets crinkling with starch, cotton slippers gliding across the verandah with a tray of whisky sours for the men, G&Ts for the women.

The Hainanese became experts on British food, able to knock up everything from toad in the hole to spotted dick. In time, they opened their own restaurants, specialising in exotic dishes such as 'Hainan-style Windsor soup,' 'Welsh rice rarebit with bull's eye egg' and, seen on a menu in Penang, 'Marmite pork chop with chips, rice and satay sauce.'

The Americans might think they invented fast food. The Chinese have been doing it for hundreds of years. Orders are shouted at an ear-splitting pitch, echoing off the white tiled walls.

Behind one stall, a small man with steamed-up glasses and a cigarette dribbling from his lower lip, scoops noodles out of a steaming cauldron.

Oil is heated in a giant wok, garlic and spices thrown in, vegetables and noodles closely following. It's all perfectly choreographed: an egg is cracked and, all in one flowing movement, the shell tossed into a far-away slops bucket. Nureyev and Fonteyn couldn't have done it better.

Next stall along, a row of yellow-skinned chicken carcasses hang down like targets in a fairground shooting alley. Chicken rice is a Hainanese speciality.

A bird is placed on a chopping board the size of a slice of tree trunk, a mighty cleaver taken in hand. A few lightening movements of the wrist and, hey presto, the beast has been sliced from backside to neck. Another few quick chops and each side of the chicken is divided into pieces and swept on to plates with rice and a dollop of chilli, with a small bowl of chicken soup placed alongside.

The *towkay* completes his ear cleaning. With one hand he's doing calculations on an abacus, fingers skipping and stroking like a virtuoso pianist. With the other he pours coffee from cup into saucer and, like a cat, takes a long, contented slurp.

"Another Black Label over here," comes the shout from the bar. Slap, slap, slap go Goldilocks' clogs.

A royal nosh-up
Brunei, 1992

Though meals in corner coffee shops and at roadside stalls are one of the joys of the region, a bit less noise and a touch of style and luxury can be seductive.

I was once invited – along with a few hundred others – to dinner at the palace of the Sultan of Brunei, at the time reputed to be the richest man in the world.

It would have been rude not to accept.

*****

The hotel lift jolts upwards. The man from Rolls-Royce, all pinstripes and shiny shoes, is shorter than me yet I still seem to be looking up his nostrils.

"Is it true," I ask, "that the Sultan has 150 Rolls-Royces?"

A pause. An adjustment of the tie, an errant piece of fluff is removed from a sleeve. The lift doors open, the seller of royal knick-knacks makes to leave.

"Naw," he says over his shoulder, a waft of aftershave filling the air. "Actually, he has 154 of them."

Brunei, perched on a slice of land on the northern coast of the island of Borneo, is a surreal, at times comical, place.

Altogether, it probably has less than 200 miles of paved roads:

that's not much tarmac to accommodate the Sultan's fleet of Rollers, let alone the Bentleys, Lamborghinis, Ferraris and other expensive runabouts he and the rest of the royal family have in their garages.

A British protectorate for nearly 100 years, Brunei became independent in 1984. It has a population of under 300,000, but an exchequer that bulges at the seams – courtesy of the country's substantial deposits of oil and gas. Sultan Hassanal Bolkiah, absolute ruler of his kingdom, sits atop this pile of cash.

We, a rag-tag group of journalists, have been flown in to help the Sultan celebrate 25 years on the throne of his small kingdom. Access to officialdom in Brunei is limited: on the other hand, not much seems to be happening.

Bandar Seri Begawan, Brunei's capital, is a pleasant, low-key sort of town, a tropical backwater where time ticks slowly by. People are relaxed but keep their heads down. The sultan is all-powerful and doesn't tolerate any opposition.

To relieve the tedium of trying to report on nothing going on, a few of us journalists go to a Chinese restaurant.

The Sultan, ex-Sandhurst, a polo-playing friend of Prince Charles and once renowned as a high-living playboy, has, on the face of it at least, become increasingly austere in his habits over the years. Alcohol is not allowed.

Fortunately, the small Chinese community that runs most of the country's commerce knows how to bend the rules.

The food arrives and a waitress in a long silk *cheongsam* appears holding two teapots. She goes from person to person.

"You want tea – or tea?" she asks. No nudges, no winks, but the message is clear.

We all opt for the teapot on the left – out of which comes foamy, cold beer, poured into small china tea cups.

For the next hour, the waitress is run ragged, her teapot constantly replenished and pouring.

There's not a sniff of alcohol about at the palace, said to be the largest royal residency in the world, taking up a substantial portion of Brunei's landmass.

The dinner guest list is impressive: a substantial dishful of foreign royalty including a mix of Malay sultans and sultanas, a layer of heads of state, with a few prime ministers added in as garnish.

There's also a sizeable stock of other dignitaries – even some ordinary people underpinning the whole affair. Altogether, a cosy 5,750 of us are gathered in the Sultan's dining room.

You either hide your wealth or flaunt it. The decor is a mix of Versailles and high season at a holiday camp. Gold leaf and brocade are everywhere. Carpets you sink into. Chandeliers the size of icebergs.

The palace has nearly 2,000 rooms, plus 300 lavatories. Italian marble covers more than 12 acres of the walls; then there are the underground garages and an adjoining polo complex, with its stud farm and air-conditioned stabling for 100 horses.

Dinner is scheduled for 7.30, but the media – noticeable for their sloppy, distinctly un-regal attire – have been told to assemble two hours earlier. Eight o'clock comes and there's no sign of food – and only over-sweetened orange juice to drink.

Koran reading competitions are a common feature of Brunei life. I once strayed into one and was buttonholed by a local who wanted to tell me all about Neil Armstrong, the astronaut and moon walker.

"When Armstrong was on the moon and about to re-enter his spacecraft, he heard a strange, beautiful sound," said my Brunei friend.

"Years later, he was visiting Cairo and, opening the window in his hotel, he listened to the muezzin in the mosque – it was the same sound he heard on the moon."

A few top table guests are shown in to the cavernous eating area. Prince Edward, representing the Queen, sits in a corner near one of the royal serving hatches. A Thai prince smiles serenely at the ceiling while, next to him, a Javanese beauty adjusts a troublesome tiara.

"G'day," says an Australian waiter, one of the more than 700 catering staff flown in for the occasion. "Not a bad little party, is it?"

He says the meat for the meal comes from the sultan's ranch in Australia – a sheep station twice the size of Brunei.

Stomachs growl. Diplomats perspire. Princesses glow.

The food finally appears. Great plates of prawns and sides of mutton, along with mountains of yellow rice, are laid out, but protocol is clear: no one can raise a fork until the Sultan gives the nod.

It's 9.45 when HRH finally arrives, his extended family – including his two wives and 10 children – in bejewelled attendance.

A royal hand reaches for the cutlery: the by now ravenous diners dig in. An over-eager Swedish cameraman hiccups, then sneezes – peppering the Japanese delegation opposite with grains of rice.

There are toasts and speeches, but the media, stuffed and over orange juiced, has had enough. The Australian waiter leads us on an escape route through the royal kitchens and out to a parking lot littered with shiny, expensive machinery.

"Trouble with you people is you have no bloody decorum," he says. We agree. Six hours of dinner is enough – even if it's with one of the richest people in the world.

Overcome by the odour
Malaysia, 1994

The olfactory senses come under constant pressure and stress in Southeast Asia – overwhelmed by spices and all manner of sauces and pastes. But of all the odours that drift around the region, nothing is quite like the smell of durian. For some, the smell and taste of what's known as the king of fruits is repugnant.

The novelist Anthony Burgess, who spent time in pre-independence Malaya teaching and writing, described eating durian as similar to consuming sweet raspberry blancmange in a lavatory.

For others, the whiff and taste give rise to a state of near orgasmic delight.

*****

Hew Choy Sam is a man on a mission.

A Malaysian Chinese with a large girth and a smile to match, he is trying to track down the tastiest durian in Southeast Asia.

"There is something very strange, almost mystical, about durians," Hew says.

A founder member of Malaysia's first-ever durian growers' association, he has a durian orchard just outside Ipoh, a quaint old tin mining town 140 miles north of Kuala Lumpur.

He smells and tastes his fruit with all the diligence of a sommelier let loose in a wine cellar. We wade through brittle long grass, cicadas supplying an orchestral backdrop.

The trees are ringed by a tall fence. There's a padlocked gate.

Hew's vocabulary is peppered with old comic-book English.

"There are rogues and scoundrels about who have nothing better to do but go round stealing durians."

Hew sharpens his *parang*, the long, all-purpose Malay knife.

"Death would be too good for those bloody rustlers."

During harvesting season in the summer months, Hew moves his bed into the orchard to guard his fruit. Some durian growers harvest their crop while it is still hanging on the tree. Hew says the fruit must be allowed to drop. Only then is the flesh guaranteed to be moist and ripe.

"I lay awake at night and count the thuds as the durians hit the ground. It is one of the most beautiful sounds you can hear."

Durians, which grow best in areas near the equator in Malaysia, Thailand and Indonesia, are temperamental fruits, easily infected by pests and disease.

The spikey outer shell gives the durian – roughly the size and shape of a US football, though considerably heavier – the look of a giant hand grenade.

"It's believed the fruit only falls at night so as not to injure people below," says Hew. "If one hits you on the head it's no laughing matter."

Inside the durian's thick outer shell is the yellow flesh round the seeds, the treasured, edible part of the fruit. It has the texture of a soft French cheese left in the sun too long.

At harvest time, durian pilgrims arrive to gorge themselves on the new crop. Faces are splattered with the fruits' golden flesh, seeds licked clean as marbles.

"People spend their lives searching for the perfect durian," says Hew, proudly pointing to one of his choice samples like a horse breeder showing off a prize-winning thoroughbred.

Prices vary widely, but durian, compared to other fruits, is top of the range. At the orchard gate, they can cost US$10 each. In Singapore, a single durian – rushed down from Malaysia while it's still fresh – might be sold for seven times that amount.

The durian has its own mythology. It aids circulation, but increases blood pressure. It's good for the complexion, but causes gout. It's an aphrodisiac, but – awkwardly – it also creates chronic wind. It must never be eaten with alcohol.

"It's not just the texture and taste of the fruit but its colour as well – and, of course, its aroma," says Hew.

Ah yes, the smell. It clings to clothes, invades every pore of the body. It's banned on airlines, trains and buses. Most hotels forbid it anywhere near the premises.

Hew says growers in Thailand – he refers to them as nincompoops – are trying to produce odourless durians in order to facilitate exports.

"You can't take the smell out of durians," he says. "For us, it's nearly as important as the taste."

The cicadas have gone quiet. The light is fading. As if on cue, there's a muffled thud as a durian hits the ground.

Doris, the great provider
Dublin, 1996

Doris, my mother-in-law, loved durians. There again, she loved most food – as long as it originated in Southeast Asia.

Born in Singapore and brought up in two cramped rooms above a corner coffee shop, Doris – her Chinese name was Seow Heng, but her husband, a film buff, nicknamed her after Doris Day – learned her cooking techniques early on.

Political upheavals, natural disasters and juicy scandals passed her by. Food was what mattered – and any wastage was a sin. Doris had a hard upbringing: in World War II, during the Japanese occupation of Singapore, she had to eat rats to survive.

Doris would visit us wherever we were based. She always took along her own provisions.

*****

The sniffer dog at Dublin airport is putting in for early retirement.

Doris has a straightforward view of the world. Singapore, where she lives, is the epicentre of all that is good when it comes to food. Expand outward from that point and, to Doris's mind, the world becomes an ever more barbaric and tasteless place.

She is visiting us in Ireland and is worried about being condemned to a diet of mushy vegetables and overdone meat. Doris's suitcase contains few clothes. Instead, there are boxes full of dried mushrooms and peppers, sweetmeats and dumplings. There are miniature bottles stuffed with cinnamon, five-spice powder, turmeric and prawn paste, plus packets of Chinese sausages and salted fish.

There's a long delay at the airport. Finally, a customs man asks me in to the arrivals hall to assist in deliberations.

Doris is sitting in a chair, an open suitcase on the table beside her.

The airport sniffer dog, a beagle in a state of severe sensory overload, is running round in tight circles.

The customs man is holding up a cellophane packet containing a flattened yellowing carcass of a bird, looking as though it's been in a collision with a Dublin Corporation steamroller.

"And what, Madam, might this be?"

Doris is shocked at such ignorance.

"Waxed duck, of course," she says. "You see, at this time of year the spring winds are blowing in China and they hang out the duck to dry. Very good for the circulation in cold weather. You cook it with…"

Any further discourse is interrupted by an almighty sneeze. The zealous customs man has made the mistake of taking the top off a bottle of Doris's home-made supercharged curry powder.

"I love a curry, but it doesn't return the compliment, if you know what I mean," says the official. "Makes the stomach do a right little jig, it does."

Doris is an expert on the digestive system.

Once, having a jittery tummy after a surfeit of chillies, she pressed a series of phials filled with what looked like ball bearings into my hand.

The accompanying leaflet explained that the bearings could cure everything from itchiness of the scalp to sweatiness of the feet. Along the way, stomach disorders would be sorted out. Every few hours, a complete phial had to poured down the throat.

Not only did the pills produce a cure. In no time I was hooked on them, emptying a couple of tubes down the throat at the slightest sign of engine room trouble.

My comeuppance came at a breakfast meeting with a group of bankers.

Feeling a little quiver in the stomach, I quickly swallowed a bunch of the little pills. Turning back to face the massed legions of moneymen, I felt a sneeze coming on.

The ball bearings, about a hundred of them, flew out like machine gun bullets.

The man from Standard Chartered ducked. The Bank of

America got a fusillade in the chest. The Bank of China watched bemused as one ball bounced, roulette wheel fashion, round his plate, finally landing with a plop in the yellow of his egg.

"Ah," said the man from the mainland, "you have diarrhoea."

I have never since gone near the pills – nor been invited to a bank managers' breakfast.

Doris is examining the custom man's face. Most people might see red cheeks as a sign of good health, but to Doris they signify a peculiar affliction called heatiness.

According to Chinese culinary traditionalists, eating is a question of maintaining a balance between opposing elements – hot and cold, sweet and sour, ying and yang. Consuming the wrong combinations of foods or downing too much strong alcohol provokes a fire inside.

She is giving more advice. "Maybe you should drink lotus root soup and some pounded tree bark to settle your digestion…"

Eventually, Doris and her culinary baggage are waved through.

"You're a very lucky woman," says the customs man, "travelling the world like you do.

"But please, next time, leave some of your spices at home," he says. "For the sake of the poor dog if for no one else."

Postscript

Miss Marple's lookalike subsequently sent me a postcard from Calcutta: "No fish heads here, but raising a glass to you and Reggie while enjoying a fiery mutton curry."

The Vatican in Kuala Lumpur has closed. Goldilocks, still dressed in his baggy shorts and singlet, is probably pouring whisky and serving chicken rice at a marble-topped bar in the sky.

The Sultan of Brunei – a few years ago he held another lavish celebration to mark 50 years on the throne – is apparently becoming ever more religious in his old age: he recently introduced strict Sharia laws, including capital punishment for homosexuals and stoning to death for women found guilty of adultery.

Under Brunei's sleepy surface, strange things have been going on: Prince Jefri, the Sultan's younger, playboy brother, was found to have misappropriated billions of dollars of state funds while serving as the country's finance minister.

Jefri, along with his collection of hundreds of cars and his extensive art collection that included a number of Modiglianis, is believed to be now confined to barracks in Brunei, while other princelings continue to live the high life in Paris, London and New York.

And there's further trouble on the horizon: there are forecasts that Brunei's oil and gas reserves – the source of the Sultan's wealth – could run out within the next decade.

Despite its smell, durian is becoming ever more popular. Consumers in China can't get enough of it and the prices keep rising. These days, you can buy durian popcorn, even durian-flavoured cappuccino. And the ever-enterprising Thais are marketing durian-flavoured condoms.

Durian has a special place in our family folklore. Back in 1995, while based in Malaysia, we were trying to adopt a child. A trunk call came through from Ipoh.

I had just written a piece for the *Financial Times* on the town's durian growers.

"Is it about durian?" I asked the voice on the other end.

"No," said the nun from the convent in Ipoh. "It's about a two-week-old boy. When are you coming to collect him?"

Dan, our youngest son, is now growing vegetables and fruit – but not durian – in the west of Ireland.

My mother-in-law Doris, Seow Heng, died at the age of 82 in Singapore in 2001. Till the last, she was boiling up soups and pounding spices. In tribute to Doris, here are two of her recipes.

Chicken rice Hainan style
(serves 4)

First, find your chicken; the bird has to be relatively small and lean, preferably corn fed. Any fat should be peeled off and set aside.

Wash and salt the inside of the chicken. Cut a generous amount of ginger and, together with a couple of spring onions, put inside the bird, sealing both ends with toothpicks.

Place the chicken in a large saucepan of boiling water. Bring to the boil again and simmer till cooked, for about 45 minutes to one hour. Take out and immerse the chicken in a basin of cold water for one minute. Drain and rub all over with sesame oil.

When the chicken has cooled, chop off the wings and thighs and halve them. Hold the carcass upright and chop straight down the breast bone, cutting each side of the chicken into two-inch pieces, leaving the flesh on the bone. Those new to the chopping business should exercise careful cleaver control at all times.

Meanwhile, wash and drain two small cups of jasmine rice. Dice a knob of ginger. Melt the fat from the chicken previously set aside and fry with the ginger briefly. Add the drained, uncooked rice and stir for a few minutes.

A rice cooker is a key part of every Asian kitchen. Empty the rice into the cooker and add a quantity of the chicken stock – the level of liquid should be one joint of the first finger above the rice. Rice takes about 20 minutes to cook.

Place the chopped chicken on a dish and pour over a mix of soy sauce, sesame oil and a small amount of chicken stock. For garnishing, use sliced cucumber and coriander. When eating, chicken pieces are usually dipped into a side sauce of pounded fresh chilli, mixed with a little lime and soy sauce.

The remaining stock, preferably sprinkled with some fried garlic, is served as a soup to accompany the meal.

Bottled chilli sauces and fried garlic are available in oriental groceries.

Malaysian fish-head curry
(serves 4)

This recipe is a little complicated, but well worth the effort. Any good Indian food shop should sell the required curry powder, spices and vegetable ingredients. If you prefer banana leaves to plates, these are also usually available in Indian groceries.

Most fishmongers sell off their fish heads cheaply – two decent-sized heads would be adequate; red mullet, salmon or cod are ideal. Ask for the heads to be cut in half and the scales and gills removed. The ones with shiny eyes are best – a sign of freshness.

Wash the heads and marinade with salt, pepper and some tamarind juice.

You'll need two tablespoons of curry powder, along with some finely-grated ginger and a teaspoon each of turmeric and coriander powder. Mix these into a paste with a small amount of water.

Cut about six ladies fingers and two aubergines into inch pieces; fry in a small amount of vegetable oil until light brown, then set aside.

Using the same oil, fry the paste along with half a dozen cloves of chopped garlic and a roughly sliced onion. Wait until the fragrance emerges, then add two sprigs of curry leaves and two chopped red chillies. Add about half a litre of water and bring to the boil.

A tin of thick coconut milk can be added at this point to thicken the mixture.

Turn down to simmer and add the fish heads and cooked vegetables. Cook slowly until the eyes of the fish go white or pop out of their sockets. Add two big tomatoes, cut into small pieces.

Serve with white rice and some liquids to put out the fire. Water or beer is best; the taste and smell of the curry tends to overwhelm wine.

CHAPTER 11:

Close shaves

Tear gas in paradise • A pole dancer puts the boot in
Laughing in the face of danger

Due to an aversion to loud bangs – and an over-developed
sense of self-preservation – I've generally avoided war
and conflict zones whenever possible. But there have been a
few close shaves.

Cycling along a track in northeast Thailand one evening
towards the tail end of the Vietnam War, a US air force B52
– returning from a bombing raid on the Ho Chi Minh trail –
dumped its surplus payload nearby. I regained consciousness
laying in a rice paddy, mangled bike 50 yards away.

In Indonesia, I was literally blown out of bed when the
military's main arsenal exploded, just down the road in the midst
of one of Jakarta's most densely-populated neighbourhoods.
Ever since, I've had a ringing sensation in one ear.

There've been a few other close encounters.

A South Pacific gassing
New Caledonia, 1985

Mr Vong, the owner of an upmarket Vietnamese restaurant in Noumea, New Caledonia's small capital, is keen to have a chat.

Over big bowls of *pho*, a Vietnamese noodle soup, he talks of his past life as a senior civil servant in Saigon and of escaping the city as Ho Chi Minh's tanks rolled in.

"And what do you do?" Mr Vong asks.

It turns out Mr Vong has an aversion to the media.

"Journalists are no good. They bring bad luck; wherever they are, they always make trouble."

The table is cleared. Shutters are drawn. The sun is shining. Yachts bob about in the turquoise waters of the harbour below. All is peaceful in the paradise islands of New Caledonia. We're on holiday, I tell Mr Vong.

Our host is not listening, shooing us out and locking the door behind us.

Mr Vong is correct. Journalists are not good news. Twenty-four hours later, the centre of Noumea is a riot zone. I end the day with lungs scorched by tear gas, vomiting into what was once an immaculately-tended town flower bed.

A number of people – rioters and police – have been shot, some believed killed. Cars and police vans are on fire, shops have been looted.

Captain Cook, ranging about the South Pacific, stumbled on this group of islands in 1774 and, seeing the misty peaks and forest valleys, named the territory after Scotland – hence, New Caledonia.

The French took the islands over in the mid-19th century, establishing a penal colony and bringing in settlers to farm the lands of the native Melanesian people, called *Kanak*. Nowadays, France maintains a big military base on New Caledonia. Each year, the French exchequer grants the territory about $1.5 billion in subsidies.

New Caledonia is a peculiar amalgam of Europe and the South Seas. Designated an overseas territory of France, the islands represent one of the most far-flung parts of the European Union, the population of 280,000 allowed to vote in both French and European parliamentary elections.

Noumea, with its tree-lined small squares where men with ample bellies play boules, feels like a town in Provence.

The trouble starts at a Bastille Day parade. Bugles sound. Crisply-dressed gendarmes salute. Then, during the singing of the *Marsellaise*, there are shouts of "Liberté".

Blue, red and green flags of the *Front de Libération National Kanak Socialist*, the local pro-independence movement, are unfurled. Stones are thrown, whistles sound.

The *Kanak* make up about 40 per cent of the population, while Europeans born on the islands – the *Caldoche* – account for just under 30 per cent, with the remainder more recent settlers from France or immigrants from other South Sea territories.

There is festering resentment about the Europeans' control over land and the islands' precious nickel deposits, which are among the world's biggest. The *Kanak* independence movement is growing in strength.

In a matter of minutes, a full-scale riot is under way, as if the streets of Paris in 1968 have been transported to the South Pacific. The sirens sing out. A phalanx of riot police appears, complete with shields, batons and face masks.

The two sides face each other in a small square of statues and sprinkling fountains. The sound of an exploding Molotov cocktail echoes off the whitewashed buildings. The first lick of tear gas drifts through the air.

New Caledonia is a favourite destination for Japanese wedding parties and honeymooners. There's a pause in proceedings as two sets of Japanese newly-weds on tandem bikes cycle across the square.

The women are in their wedding dresses, the men in tails,

charmingly oblivious to the mayhem around them.

They exit left and the rioting resumes, moving down to the harbour. An officer shouts through a bullhorn for the crowds to disperse. No one takes any notice.

Volley after volley of tear gas is fired.

A large cruise ship is navigating its way towards the dockside. Flowery shirts and billowing dresses line the decks. The water churns: the ship has decided that, for today at least, Noumea is not a desirable tourist destination. With a mournful hoot, the vessel and its passengers turn about and head out to sea.

The line of riot police advances. A tear gas canister hits my leg and I'm on the ground, breathing in acrid white smoke. My notebook scoots across the cobbles and falls into the water.

Tear gas doesn't kill you, but it has a good try: my face is on fire, the lungs feel as though they're home to an infestation of red ants.

A group of *Caldoche*, armed with iron bars and what look like baseball bats, pull me away. One, a wiry man with crazed eyes, is carrying a pistol and baying for *Kanak* blood.

I escape my saviours. The boutiques of central Noumea are boarded up. Glass, along with abandoned flip flops, litters the streets. A palm tree lies across the road like a giant toilet brush.

The next day, I pass by Mr Vong's restaurant. Pro-independence graffiti has been daubed on the shutters. The man himself is nowhere to be seen.

Blood in the beer
Uzbekistan, 2004

Some cities welcome you with open arms, some shrug their shoulders indifferently, others are hostile and forbidding.

On a cold, grey October day, Tashkent, the capital of the Republic of Uzbekistan in Central Asia, is not a friendly-looking place.

Officials at the airport are gruff, tossing my passport from desk to desk, running fingers over the harp on the cover, each stamp and visa examined and queried.

Leaving the airport, the taxi driver is catatonic – except when demanding a fistful of dollars. It's early evening by the time I reach the hotel.

*****

The lobby is as welcoming as a funeral parlour. A receptionist paints her nails. The porter, head on desk, lets out an occasional snore. A fat man in a misshapen suit sits on a purple sofa, pudgy hands on belly, staring into space and making loud sucking noises through his teeth.

Outside the plate glass door, a searchlight criss-crosses the sky. Snow is beginning to fall.

"Sunshine Club, fifth floor," says the sign. Time to see what the Uzbeks get up to in the evenings.

Uzbekistan is one of the poorest countries in Central Asia. Since independence from the old Soviet Union in 1991, its economy has gone into freefall. The landscape is littered with rusting, tumbledown Soviet-era factories.

Islam Karimov, the head of state, is all-powerful and it's best to watch your step. It's rumoured that Karimov – his family and friends run the place like a private fiefdom – is partial to submerging political opponents in boiling vats of water.

A babushka at the night club's reception desk, face like a clenched fist and dressed head to toe in black, demands my coat. A docket is filled in, a numbered tag handed over.

Obviously, it's one of Tashkent's quieter evenings. I am the Sunshine Club's only customer. A lonely loop of coloured lights trails round the dimly-lit room. A trim young man orders me to a table. Without any questions, a beer is brought: it's chilled to near ice, the cold of the glass sticking to my hand.

Inflation is rampant in Uzbekistan. The local currency – the Som – is best counted by the inch rather than by the note. A thick wodge is handed over. A sip or two and I'm about to leave, but then there's a whiff of perfume and a glimpse of an elegant midriff, covered in goosebumps.

A pole dancer is at, or rather on, the table.

Apart from carefully-managed groups who visit fabled sites such as Samarkand and Bukhara, Uzbekistan is not on the tourist map.

Tashkent – much of the city was destroyed in a massive earthquake in the mid-1960s – is full of stern-looking office buildings, along with line upon line of glum apartment buildings, the so-called Khrushchev blocks that sprout like concrete mushrooms all over the former Soviet Union.

Sitting there among the fairy lights, I feel a little ridiculous, unable to avert my eyes from what's happening inches in front of me. The legs of the boots, which stretch ever upwards, are made of shiny black plastic.

The footwear is stout, more suited to coal mining than nightclub dancing. The boots have built-up, thick wooden soles: the pointed toe of each is edged with a strip of shiny, aggressive-looking silvery metal.

The majority of Uzbekistan's population is Muslim. Would the country's religious leaders approve of what's going on? I lean forward to take a gulp of beer.

Rock music booms out. A strobe light darts round the room. The pole dancer is speeding up, swinging round like a dervish. Sipping my drink, I suddenly feel a stinging pain in my temple, just by the eye.

The beer is turning red. Blobs of blood fall on the vinyl-topped table.

Galyna is beautiful. She is from Odessa in Ukraine. Her name means calm. Her father has a collapsed lung and she is in Uzbekistan trying to save money to send home.

All this I find out later. Now she is sobbing, cradling my head. There are cloths and hot water. The waiter, Galyna's boyfriend, is a medical student from Kiev and has calmly taken charge. He has an excellent bedside manner.

"It is only a small cut," he says. "A lot of blood, but it is only..." – he pauses, searching for the correct medical term – "superfacial."

The mind drifts. A headline floats into view: 'Journalist killed in pole dancing mystery'.

Galyna is shivering: she has green, slightly oriental eyes. The babushka is there, transformed. She's leaning over me, gently stroking my hand.

Who is going to explain this to my wife and family? Will people laugh or cry?

And who will describe the art of pole dancing to my mother?

The medical student insists I swallow a cup of strong, black tea. He dresses the wound and applies a plaster.

Three pairs of eyes look at me in supplication. On no account should the hotel management hear of the incident. At the very least, everyone would lose their jobs.

I'm grateful to be alive and have no wish to deliver Galyna and the others up to President Karimov's bubbling pots. And I'll stay well clear of nightclubs in future.

Air of high anxiety
Lagos, Nigeria, 2005

The airline trade says the odds of being killed in an air crash are next to zero. Car crashes, choking on a fish bone, being brained by a stray coconut are far more liable to send you on to the other world.

Yet flying does have its moments, even when it feels as if the end is only a wing tip away.

*****

The first sign of trouble is a muffled explosion, followed by a grating, turbulent sound, as if an industrial-sized dishwasher has gone berserk.

Outside the window, the shells of abandoned planes, their silvery carcasses covered in green mold, go by in a blur. The aircraft is at full pelt, just about to lift off.

Seatbelts strain against bellies as the engines are flung into reverse. Clouds of white smoke appear outside as the brakes are slammed on.

Wahala is a term used in Nigeria to denote trouble or stress. Lagos has *wahala* in bucketfuls. With its population of anywhere between 13 and 16 million – no one is entirely sure of the number – the city is one of those places where you wonder just how anything manages to function.

Built on a swamp and a series of islands, the city is sinking. There's no mass transit system, no proper sewage network, a power supply that's more off than on, and potable water for only a few.

The ornate red hat of the man on one side of me skips off down the aircraft cabin, closely followed by a food trolley, a stack of newspapers and, strangest sight of all, roll after flying roll of toilet paper.

My friend Ibim, a local journalist intent on showing me what she calls "the real Nigeria" far away from Lagos, grabs my thigh in a blood-stopping clasp. We come to a halt with one last rodeo-style lurch, less than 100 yards from a settlement of shanty houses at the end of the runway. The smell of burning tyre rubber fills the air.

Nigerians are well used to coping with the unexpected. There are no screams, no tears. Instead, after a few seconds silence, someone at the back of the plane starts laughing. Before long, everyone's at it, as if the locals have decided the only way to combat the haphazard, often frightening world they inhabit is with bellyfuls of humour.

A hostess returns the red hat to the man next to me and gathers up the toilet rolls.

We limp back to the terminal. "Welcome to Nigeria, the happiest country in Africa," says a sign. "Mind the roof," says another placard further along.

The pilot – he has a Russian accent and proudly enunciates each syllable of his English with meticulous care – says there's been a bird strike.

"I give you great apologies. I am sorry for your worry. Please to be careful later."

As we come down the aircraft steps, a gaggle of airport staff are peering up at one of the engines: apparently it's been totally wrecked.

Amidst all the chaos of Lagos – the potholes, the blackouts, the constant hooting of horns, the piles of rubbish – there's a vibrant energy about the city. In 1991, the capital was moved from Lagos to the far more orderly new administrative centre of Abuja.

All over Lagos there are abandoned, ugly hulks of what were once central government offices and ministries. During the week, civil servants sit in their new premises in Abuja, but, come the weekend, they scurry back to the sinking city by the sea, craving its disorder and madness.

At the airport terminal, people fall into that easy-going, tactile form of familiarity that is second nature to Nigerians.

Make-up is applied. Elaborate dresses adjusted. Men with large tummies ruminate over business deals. Family connections are discussed, the government condemned.

"That blaggard of a governor – he was supposed to build a hospital, but bought himself a new jet instead," says one big belly.

"Yes, but his new young wife will probably kill him," says another. Cue a bout of thigh-slapping laughter. Humour and an attitude of optimistic fatalism are the lubricants that make the chaos bearable and keep life turning.

Sit in a Lagos traffic jam and look at the dented yellow buses, crammed with passengers, that limp and belch their way round the city. All have messages carefully etched on them.

"Such is life," says one, "No Tension," says another, with horn blaring.

A particularly rusty wagon, its exhaust trailing a dense cloud of blue smoke, strikes a more philosophical note. "The downfall of man is not the end of his life," is scrawled along its battered side.

Such is the state of Lagos traffic – it's not unusual for people to spend six hours getting to and from work each day – that many people don't bother with going shopping. Instead, the shops come to them.

You can buy everything you need from hawkers who patrol the queues of buses, cars and trucks. Want a curtain rail? No problem, just wind down the window. A mirror? Your groceries? A book, a chair, lampshade or bed? It's all there in the midst of the choking traffic.

Back at the airport, there's an announcement.

"The replacement aircraft is being serviced," says a cheery voice. "You'll be on your way just as soon as we've managed to put the plane back together."

Ibim once again grabs my thigh in a vice-like grip, bent forward with laughter. Others are similarly convulsed, tears streaming down faces.

"You see," says Ibim. "All this *wahala* – that's Nigeria for you."

We did fly off in the end.

Postscript

The divide between New Caledonia's *Kanak* and *Caldoche* communities deepened in subsequent years, with more outbreaks of violence.

Nineteen *Kanak* separatists and six police and soldiers were killed in a hostage shootout in 1988.

Tensions remain high. A number of referenda have been held in recent years on whether the territory should become independent. The result of the latest poll, held in late 2021, was overwhelmingly in favour of remaining part of France, although most Kanaks refused to recognise the legitimacy of the vote and boycotted proceedings.

A friend who visited Noumea some years back reported that Mr Vong's restaurant had closed and its owner had left, last heard of back in Saigon, making a fortune in the coffee business.

Galyna has probably moved on from life as a pole dancer. I only hope she and her boyfriend escaped the barbarity and slaughter inflicted on Ukraine, their homeland.

Not long after the close encounter with Galyna's boot, I was sent to Northampton to report on the decline of what was once the city's shoe manufacturing business.

In the workshop of one of the few remaining shoe factories, an embarrassed manager pointed to the firm's latest, highly-lucrative, fashion line – elaborate variations of Galyna's footwear. A film on the subject, *Kinky Boots*, became a great hit.

Islam Karimov, Uzbekistan's dictator, died in 2016. Some political prisoners were subsequently released, but while government opponents might no longer be boiled alive, the Tashkent regime remains one of the most repressive in the world.

In the 1990s and early 2000s, aircraft in Nigeria would regularly drop out of the sky. Though safety has improved in recent years, air travel in the country still presents considerable challenges.

A few years ago, Nigeria's biggest airline, notorious for its bad service, had to be rescued from bankruptcy by the government. Officials said the decision was taken "to instill sanity in the aviation sector and prevent a major catastrophe".

CHAPTER 12

And the closing headlines . . .

"A WISE MAN IS KNOWN BY THE FEWNESS OF HIS WORDS."
– Rule of St Benedict

Kibbutz Gal-on, the settlement on the edge of the Negev desert in Israel where I wrote my first, ill-fated journalistic article, is still operating, though much has changed.

As Israel has developed, the old communal ideals of kibbutz life have been replaced by more individualistic, capitalistic ways.

I've never been back, but a friend who returned talked of a demographic crisis as young kibbutzniks left for the city. In the old days, all decisions were made by settlers' committees. Now there are managers and flow charts.

Naomi, the young soldier who sang patriotic songs in the apple orchards, fought in the Six Day War but subsequently turned her back on the military, the soldier boyfriend and the rugged kibbutz existence and went to live in an artists' colony in the hills of Galilee.

I've managed to miss some big stories over the years: sleeping through a coup d'état in Thailand; sitting on a plane out of

Georgia on the day the Russians invaded; drinking in a bar in Köln as the Berlin Wall fell; and – more than half a century ago – leaving Israel the day before war broke out.

Wise people say you shouldn't regret what you have done; it's what you didn't do that really matters. Top of my list in that department is the chance I missed – due to a mix-up over dates – of an interview with Nina Simone at her home in the south of France shortly before she died. That still hurts.

But then there have been the good times, those magic occasions that make you feel you're really living.

Dancing the night away in Havana and meeting the Pope in Papua New Guinea rate pretty highly. At the other end of the scale, that near-death experience from the boot of a pole dancer in a Tashkent nightclub is one to tell the grandchildren.

A stranger summed it up best.

It's a normal summer's day in the west of Ireland. A belt of sand whips along the beach, shingle breathing in and out as the waves pound the shore; a bank of black clouds puffs up on the Atlantic horizon, a giant's army on the charge.

The water is ridiculously cold.

A head, bald as a newly-peeled onion, bobs up in the waves beside me.

"I saw youse runnin' down the shore and I says to the wife, I'm goin' in. She says I'm mad, but jeez now, isn't it great?"

He leaps up, body arching, waves thrashing at white flesh.

"It all makes you feel feckin' alive."

And that, feeling feckin' alive, is what it's all about.

Acknowledgements

This book would not have come into being without the insistence of family members. "Please, no more telling stories – just write it all down," they said. So here it is. As always, my love to Gene, Christy and Dan.

Many others have helped along the way.

John Kamm, of the Dui Hua Foundation, and the late Tom Gorman played leading roles in the China expedition and steered me in and out of trouble.

Lesley Nelson provided a floor to sleep on, and several memorable Soho experiences.

Peter Millership was the source of lavish hospitality in Jakarta.

Jackie Willcox and Peter Mackridge, Emeritus Professor of Modern Greek at Oxford, gave invaluable advice and shared many fun-filled times in Greece.

Maria Becket took me on several unforgettable journeys around the world. Thanks to Jim Becket and to Daphne, his and Maria's daughter, for supplying details of Maria's rich and varied life.

André Aciman gave encouragement: thanks to him for

allowing quotation from his captivating book on Ladino family life, *Out of Egypt*, published by Faber & Faber.

In Ireland, thanks and respects to the Gaffney family in Louisburgh, and to Jerry Cowley, of the Safe Home scheme. Thanks also to Peter Shanley, in Westport, for leading me to Wittgenstein's chickens.

Thanks to Michael Longley for allowing quotation of his poem on Charlie Gaffney, contained in his collection *A Hundred Doors* (Vintage Publishing).

Gratitude to Monsignor T for his advice on clerical clothing, and to Father Tom for enriching the Cuba experience.

In California, respect is due to Frank Green and his wife Diana for taking a risk and allowing me to marry them.

In Nigeria, Ibim Semenitari was the inspiration for many adventures, some frightening but always full of laughter.

I owe Ian Richardson, a former editor at BBC World Service radio and TV, a good lunch for his advice and encouragement.

Both poems by Katerina Anghelaki-Rooke – *The Scar* and *Aegina 1* – appear in the collection *From Purple Into Night* (Shoestring Press), translated into English by Katerina and Jackie Willcox; the latter gave kind permission for their quotation.

The Six Month Kingdom, by Duncan Heaton-Armstrong, is published by I.B. Tauris.

A House for Mr Biswas, by V.S. Naipaul, was first published by André Deutsch.

Some of the events appearing here were adapted for the feature pages of the *Financial Times*, *The Independent* and *The Irish Times* or were broadcast on the BBC and RTE. I'm grateful to these organisations for giving the stories an airing.

Ben Burt, ace accordion player and anthropologist, made corrections and many useful suggestions

Dave Clare and John Houston have played a vital role: they gave me a sharp but encouraging kick to finish the writing and enable them to put this book together.

Dave, great grandson of an emigrant Mayo shoemaker who eventually died in a Liverpool workhouse, is a veteran sub-editor and production editor. He worked for many years on *The Guardian*, having started out as a trainee news reporter on a Lancashire weekly paper in the days when many 'local rag' front pages were solely for adverts.

John is an art editor who worked for many years at *The Observer* and *The Guardian*. Among his many creations was a famous Gone With the Wind poster parody in 1985, substituting Ronald Reagan and Margaret Thatcher for Clark Gable and Vivien Leigh, with a caption that read: "She promised to follow him to the end of the earth. He promised to organise it."